MONEY MANAGEMENT

For Busy People

Monty McKinnon

Edited by

Thom Corbett

Master Financial Planning Services Inc.
Box 131, Newmarket, ON L3Y 4W3

MASTER FINANCIAL PLANNING SERVICES INC.
P.O. Box 131, Newmarket, Ontario L3Y 4W3

Money Management
For Busy People

All rights reserved. Published October, 1990 First Edition

Printed in Canada by Harmony Printing Limited

Cover copy and concept by Univision Marketing Group Ltd.

ISBN 0-9693761-1-1

Unless otherwise stated scriptutes quoted are from:

Scripture is taken from the Holy Bible: New International Version, copyright 1973, 1978, 1984 by the International Bible Society. Used by permission of Zondervan Bible Publishers.

Scripture is taken from the New American Standard Bible, 1960, 1962, 1963, 1968, 1971, 1972, 1973, 1975, 1977 The Lockman Foundation. Used by permission.

An effort has been made to acknowledge all sources used in this material. If inadvertently and source has been omitted, please advise our organization and any error will be corrected in future publications

Other Books Available

What Every Christian Should Know About Money Management

Dedication

One day I realized my life was meaningless and full of turmoil. I was going nowhere in a hurry. It was then, I realized that I needed the Lord.

I am grateful to the Lord for the exceptional favour He has given me. Clearly, I can see no other way to live than to place Him first in my life. When Jesus became Lord of my life, He changed me for the better. The last ten years have been the most significant and important years for me, and I owe it all to Jesus.

I cheerfully and humbly dedicate this book to my Lord, Jesus Christ, and thank Him for allowing me the privilege to present this material on finances.

Acknowledgements

I would like to acknowledge the support and help given me by my associates, friends, my children, Peter, Emily and especially my wife, Donna.

In particular, I offer my thanks and genuine gratitude to Mr. Thom Corbett for his encouragement and for lending me his editing skills. Thanks to my brother Bruce, Erusin, Duane, Susan, and my wife Donna for all their help in proof reading.

Thanks to Victor Woodhouse, Woodhouse Executive Insurance; Wendy Collard of Royal LePage, Willowdale; Bob Luery, Remax, Newmarket and Bryan Sykes B. Com., C.A., George Smith & Co., Newmarket, their support and input is much appreciated.

A special thanks to all the people who have invited me into their homes during the past ten years and allowed me the privilege to assist them with their finances. This book is the result of those visits.

My goal is to help the individual Christian as well as Christian organizations become free from debt. Hopefully, this book will spark some interest and encourage better money management.

Special Acknowldegement

A number of ministries and book stores need to be recognized for their out standing spirit of co-operation in helping with the distribution of this book. Campus Crusade For Christ Of Canada, Crossroads Christian Communications Inc. (100 Huntley Street), World Vision Canada, The Peoples Church Toronto.

Preface

For over a decade, I have been privileged to use my gifts to counsel thousands of people in the area of financial planning. It has been rewarding to illustrate God-given financial principles that ensure money can be a blessing and not a burden. They all had one thing in common, to be better stewards of God's resources.

During this time, I have seen a variety of situations ranging from not so bad to horrendous. The most common problem has been a failure to prepare a family budget. I have spent time with families who are so deep in debt they see no other way out but through declaring bankruptcy. Of course there is an alternative, handling finances based on biblical principles.

Discussing with elderly couples how their money would be spent after they died. They wanted to honour God and ensure their family and several charities would receive the bulk of their estate. They knew this would not happen unless they had a Will.

Those who read my first book (What Every Christian Should Know About Money Management) were asking me for more tips on handling their money so that they could honour God in the financial area of their life. This book is an attempt to answer some of their many questions.

This is also a book about options. Options for people who are so deep in debt their whole life has become a nightmare. Options for people who have been blessed with great wealth but are not sure how they can honour God with their resources.

This book is an attempt to provide Christians with a roadmap through some of the financial difficulties we all face. A roadmap from the Provider of everything we have. A roadmap to keep others from repeating the financial mistakes so many have made in the past.

This book is not intended for late night reading. It was written for doing. Just as the scriptures talk of the person who looks into a mirror only to forget what they look like after walking away, a similar danger exists for "readers" of this book.

Through following the principles contained in both my previous book and this book, completing the exercises and discussing them with your family, you will soon be on the road to financial security. A security that comes from being debt free while sharing your wealth with others.

Success in the financial area of our life requires establishing correct priorities, making a plan and perseverance. The final and perhaps the most important element is commitment. Success always follows commitment.

Foreward

Monty McKinnon's first book, *"What Every Christian Should Know About Money Management"*, was distributed to partners and viewers of "100 Huntley Street." It proved to be a valuable resource for many who were struggling financially or just needed guidance in planning for the future.

The positive feedback we received about the book reinforced our belief that there is a need for such material in today's Christian community – a need which I'm sure still exists.

Now *"Money Management For Busy People"* addresses a wider range of money matters and answers questions not covered in the scope of the first book.

God has gifted Monty with tremendous wisdom in the area of finances. His clear and practical insights not only give sound financial guidance but Bible-based principles on which to govern this area of our lives. It changes our whole perspective on money to realize that God is the ultimate provider of all we have and that He expects us to good stewards of it.

You will want to keep this book in a handy place and refer to it as your financial questions arise. I trust that this book will be a blessing as you apply its principles and put God first in your finances (Matthew 6:33).

David Mainse
Host of "100 Huntley Street"

Table of Contents

About The Material In This Book

The articles in this book, represent information and suggestions about specific financial topics in everyone's life. In some cases, a sequential learning plan is provided which Donna and I practice in our own lives. The reader is encouraged to study further any article of interest before making any changes to their financial situation.

The statistical and factual information contained in the book is obtained from reputable sources, including the governments of the Provinces of Canada. As such, this material is to be considered accurate at the time of publication and Master Financial Planning Services Inc., including its' directors and staff cannot accept responsibility for subsequent changes in information or errors found concerning this publication or the sources used.

Master Financial Planning Services Inc. and it's representatives are not engaged in rendering legal, accounting, investment advisory or other professional service. The advice and recommendations contained here are based upon our analysis of the situation as it presently exists. While most of these concepts are unlikely to be affected by financial events in the near future, some changes, for example, in taxation, GST, or other areas may require the reader to obtain updated recommendations from his/her financial advisor.

The information provided herewith, whether composed of computer software illustrations, analyses, reports, hand written/drawn illustrations, brochures, prototypes/specimen documentation etc., are entirely for educational purposes.

While great care has been taken to ensure the accuracy of the statements and information contained in our publication, no liability is assumed for financial or legal decisions based upon the contents of this book.

The Easy Way
Or The Right Way?

1

The Easy Way Or The Right Way

Regardless of your income, it is better for you to control your finances than have your finances control you. We are reminded in the Bible that we are to control ourselves and subsequently our expenditures. (Pr. 29:11b) We are further reminded that if we lose control of our spending, the borrower becomes the servant of the lender. (Pr.22:7)

Preparing a proper financial plan is wise. In fact, there is further evidence found in Titus 3:8 giving support to the idea of controlling finances. "This is a trustworthy saying. And I want you to stress these things, so that those who have trusted in God may be careful to devote themselves to doing what is good. These things are excellent and profitable for everyone."

In order to help us stay on track, we need to be familiar with the more common mistakes we make when handling money. Although some mistakes are more serious than others, the following list is in no particular order of severity. While our record contains the most common mistakes, they are usually the easiest to correct.

Common Mistakes

1. Not having a written financial plan
2. Not setting any financial goals
3. Not having a family budget
4. Not keeping accurate financial records
5. Not planning for retirement
6. Not having adequate life insurance protection
7. Not giving a tithe to charity
8. Not establishing an emergency fund
9. Not contributing to a savings program
10. Not buying items on sale
11. Not managing credit spending
12. Not making contributions to retire a home mortgage
13. Not seeking professional help
14. Not preparing a Will
15. Not making a gift to charity in your Will
16. Not reviewing your Will regularly
17. Not shopping for the lowest interest rate for credit purchases
18. Not shopping for the best interest rate for your investments
19. Not investigating before investing
20. Not keeping more of your tax dollars
21. Not borrowing for the correct reasons
22. Not learning more about financial matters
23. Not allowing flexibility in budgeting matters
24. Not involving the family in financial concerns and projects
25. Not being accountable for your spending

Keeping Financially Fit

2

Financial Fitness

Financial fitness does not guarantee success and happiness. The road to monetary health, begins with the premise that all Christians should have a financial plan.

Your financial plan is a blueprint of your resources today and a map of where you are going financially. Happiness is not found at the end of the journey, rather, it is found along the route. A financial plan provides the peace of mind that comes from knowing you are able to afford the lifestyle you enjoy while ensuring that your resources are working for you.

Financial fitness requires effort on our part. It requires planning, reviewing your plans, making changes when necessary and following through on commitments. It also involves a team effort. The Bible is quite clear on the principle of unity. People who establish enormous goals seldom achieve those goals by themselves. They have help. Clear agreement within your family or team members, enables you to reach or exceed your goals.

Fortunately, we don't have to go it alone—even if you are single, widow or widower, you have an advisor and friend. This friend has the ultimate wisdom, he is faithful, and closer than a brother. His name is Jesus. Invite Him to become your friend and a member of your team. Success in the financial areas of our lives require us to establish correct priorities, especially if we want to be blessed by the Lord. That is why He reminds us to seek His kingdom and righteousness first, after which He will meet our needs. (Mt.6:33) Clearly, we must put Jesus first and foremost in our daily lives.

As with physical fitness, the key to successful financial fitness is to obtain a financial check-up before implementing a slow, cautious exercise program. By using the resources you have and working to see them grow, you begin to feel better. Your new healthy state of financial fitness helps you cope with stress while allowing you to stretch yourself in times of need without causing injury. As with physical fitness, each step you take leads to a higher level of fitness.

Whenever you decide to do something significant, you will experience opposition. You can expect some people to express jealousy, anger, and envy as you strive to become financially fit.

Intelligence

The financial marketplace appears to be confusing and difficult, especially when you view the stock exchange. On the floor of the exchange, traders yell at one another in what appears to be total chaos. Yet underneath the apparent chaos, million-dollar transactions are occurring. Experienced and knowledgeable traders thrive in what they consider order.

The Bible teaches us to seek knowledge, understanding and wisdom. If we are to become financially fit, we must rely on the Lord. "For the Lord gives wisdom, and from His mouth comes knowledge and understanding." (Pr.2:6)

Financial fitness requires us to educate ourselves and gain experience in areas of finance that interest us. We can learn from magazines, newspapers, books, night school, correspondence courses, and Bible study. There is another source which is often overlooked, probably because it is so obvious we take the source for granted; "And I will give you pastors according to mine heart, which shall feed you with knowledge and understanding."(Je.3:15)

In addition to technical resources and pastors, God has given each of us a good measure of common sense. Some people use it and others never develop this talent. Common sense can be developed through use. As we make decisions, right or wrong, we learn, we grow and improve. Our decisions, however, must be made in the context of Scriptural principles, acknowledging that "all scripture is God-breathed and is useful for teaching, rebuking, correcting and training in righteousness." (2 Tim. 3:16)

Time

Have you ever noticed, regardless of how much time you set aside for a certain job, it always seems to take longer? Have you noticed what happens when we eat too much of the wrong food and how quickly we gain weight? When we try to lose those unwanted pounds, however, it becomes a long and strenuous task.

Consider what happens when we shop with a credit card? While it's quite easy to spend too much money and wind up in debt, it can take a long time to pay it all off.

Financial fitness doesn't happen overnight. It is often a long program of learning and applying the knowledge we gain to improve our situation.

We should not place undue pressure on ourselves to resolve a problem which may have taken months or years to develop. Through proper planning and wise counsel we will soon see light at the end of the tunnel.

If you don't think time is important, examine what happens to your RRSP over 10, 20 or 30 years. It is amazing to see how time and compounding interest can work for your benefit. God's timing is always perfect if we seek Him throughout all of our financial planning.

Budgeting, The Key To Success

3

Does this sound familiar? You sit down and write out a detailed budget. In a few short weeks or months however, you and other members of the family are not following anything contained in the budget? Why does this happen so often? We have good intentions, but, nothing seems to get done.

Budgets are important. They are a practical demonstration of a plan and planning is a Biblical principal. It is unwise to consider a project without calculating whether we have the resources to complete the task.(Lk.14:28) A budget is a guide which will help us become accountable and accountability is important to God. (Lk.16.2)

It Is A Matter Of Attitude

If you were to visit some of your closest friends, your boss, co-workers, and ask them or your family to rate your attitude, how do you think you would score? Would you be viewed as someone who is challenged by the excitement of life and always ready to persevere. Or would you be viewed as a dismal failure in the adventure of life?

Attitude is what separates the winners from the losers. All too often we allow our environment to shape our attitude instead of our attitude shaping our environment. Consider what Paul had to say:

"Finally, brothers, whatever is true, whatever is noble, whatever is right, whatever is pure, whatever is lovely, whatever is admirable—if anything is excellent or praiseworthy—think about such things." (Phil. 4:8)

When we approach a problem with the right attitude, we will usually succeed in finding a solution to the problem. The right attitude is a matter of choice. We either choose to be successful and work hard at resolving our financial difficulties, or we choose to ignore them and hope they will go away.

The development and maintenance of a family budget is important. It not only reflects your attitude concerning financial matters, it also sets you free from debt.

I find it interesting that we will spend more time this week in front of our television, than in preparing for our financial future. How is it that we neglect such an important element of financial success?

When we go to work, our boss might require us to prepare departmental or division budgets for the coming year, and we do it. So, it's not that we don't know how to prepare a budget. Could it be that we are lazy, embarrassed, feel restricted, procrastinate, or are too frightened to make a commitment to change.

A Helpful Tool

A budget is a helpful tool. More than that, it is a biblical principle. (Lk.14:28-30; Pr.24:3,4.) The purpose of a budget is to provide a guidance system that will send out alarm signals if we are heading in the wrong direction. A proper budget needs flexibility and the ability to deal with emergencies.

Procrastination is the number one enemy. Putting off the decision to implement a budget is not one of the problems, it is the problem. We tend to put off drawing up a budget because we perceive ourselves to be too busy. We also feel that a budget is for those who have financial trouble. Ironically the opposite is true. A budget can get you out of debt or it can keep you out of debt in the first place.

A budget should not require more than thirty minutes a week for updating and reporting on your progress. If the budget becomes time consuming or burdensome, it is probably too detailed and should be refined. Budgeting should involve all family members. This includes the drawing up of a budget and a commitment from all family members to live within the agreed limits.

Creating A Successful Budget

Creating a successful budget is not difficult. Review the following easy steps that will help you control your money instead of your money controlling you.

- Analyze your present situation
- Determine where you might reduce spending
- Consider your total income
- Prepare a budget based on your necessary expenses
- Adjust until balanced

Analysis Of Present Situation

We need to know where we are coming from before we can determine where we are heading. Complete the Personal Asset Form. This will provide a snapshot of your current situation. Regardless of your financial condition, you should complete this form. There is an extra copy at the back of the book which you can edit to meet your needs.

Determine Necessary Expenses

For our budget process, we will consider those expenses which the family has determined as being necessary. Divide expenses into two groups, either fixed or variable expenses. The heart of budgeting is to determine which expenses are of a fixed nature (those that must be paid and do not vary in amounts) and those expenses which are variable (those that have no fixed payment or amount).

While the following list offers typical fixed and variable expenses, it may not totally be complete or specific to your situation. Add or delete from the list until you have a personal and complete list of your fixed expenses.

What you have formulated is an outline of your family budget. It may need to be modified slightly and it will likely change over time.

Do not allow yourself to become sloppy and neglect keeping accurate records. Remember, as a steward, we will all have to give an accounting of our stewardship. (Lk 16:1,2) What is important is not how much we have but what we do with what we have been given.

SUMMARY ASSET EVALUATION FORM

ASSETS		LIABILITIES	
Chequing Accounts	$ _____	Bank Loans	$ _____
Savings Accounts	_____	Charge Accounts	_____
Life Ins. Cash Value	_____	Monthly Bills O/S	_____
Money Owed You	_____	Other	_____
Gold/Silver	_____		
Securities	_____	*Mortgages*	_____
Stocks	_____	Home	_____
Canada Savings Bonds	_____	Cottage	_____
Mutual Funds	_____	Other	_____
Term Deposits	_____		
Business	_____	Debts/Individuals	_____
Other	_____	Credit Unions	_____
		Personal Property Loans _____	
Automobiles	_____	Automobiles	_____
House Funishings	_____	Rec. Vehicles	_____
Antiques/Jewelry	_____	Other	_____
Real Estate	_____		
Home	_____	TOTAL LIABILITIY $ _____	
Cottage	_____		
Condo	_____		
Other	_____		
Pension	_____	*NET WORTH*	_____
Company	_____		
RRSP's	_____	Total Assets	$ _____
Annuities	_____	Less	_____
Insurance Face Value	_____	Total Liabilities	$ _____
Insurance FV Spouse	_____		
Other	_____	Net Estate	$ _____
TOTAL ASSETS	$ _____	Dated _____	

Anticipated Expenses

Fixed Expenses

Tithe _____

Rent/Mortgage _____

Insurance _____

Bank Loans _____

Health Insurance _____

Saving Program _____

Emergency Fund _____

Other _____

Total Fixed Expenses $ _____

Variable Expenses

_____

Food (At Home,Restaurants) _____

Transportation (Ins., Gas, Fares) _____

Clothing _____

Recreation _____

Vacations _____

Utilities (Heat, Hydro, Water) _____

Home Improvements _____

Other _____

Other _____

Total Variable Expenses $ _____

Total Expenditures $ _____

Consider Total Amount Of Income

Determine all sources of income from both you and your spouse. Do not include possible salary adjustments or bonuses in the coming year.

SOURCES OF ANNUAL INCOME

Annual Family Total

Present employment   _____
Spousal employment   _____
Part-time employment   _____
Investments   _____
Interest on money invested _____
Money owed you   _____
Pension Company   _____
Pension Private   _____
Annuities   _____
RRIF   _____
Canada Pension   _____
Old Age Security   _____
Canada Pension Supplements _____
Rental Income   _____
Other   _____

TOTAL INCOME $ _____

THE FAMILY BUDGET

INCOME

Present Employment	_____
Spousal Employment	_____
Part-Time Employment	_____
Investment Interest	_____
Interest On Money Invested	_____
Money Owed You	_____
Pension Company	_____
Private Pension	_____
Annuities	_____
RRIF	_____
Canada Pension	_____
Old Age Security	_____
Canada Pension Supplements	_____
Rental Income	_____
Other	_____
TOTAL INCOME	$ _____

EXPENSES

Food	$ _____
Shelter	_____
Transportation	_____
Emergency Fund	_____
Entertainment	_____
Recreation	_____
Security	_____
Charitable Donations	_____
Utilities	_____
Taxes	_____
Debt Payment	_____
Investments	_____
Medical Expenses	_____
Clothing	_____
Personal	_____
Other	_____
TOTAL EXPENSES	$ _____

In contrasting an athlete with the Christian "runner", Paul makes it clear that the key elements to success are discipline and single-minded perseverance. (1Co.9:24-27) Once we make our commitment, we must be prepared to press on to the goal of financial freedom.

At the same time, all planning and subsequent goals and objectives should be subject to frequent review. If necessary, changes can and should be made during the process. This ensures that the budget will not become impossible to follow.

The personal commitment that you and your family bring to the budgeting process is crucial to its success or failure. You should also seek good counsel in all decision-making. While discipline is necessary for adhering to your decisions, avoid being slavish to a plan that has been made redundant by changing circumstances.

A proper budget will enable you to determine how you should spend your money and where you can save money. It is not restricting, in fact it will allow you to be better informed while enabling you to make intelligent decisions concerning financial matters.

Of course, none of this will happen unless you take the first step and prepare a budget.

Preparing For Financial Emergencies

4

With the number of times we face a financial emergency in our lifetime, it's surprising that more of us don't have an emergency fund. Without such a fund, an unexpected problem can place a major stress on our financial resources. The Bible teaches us in 2Ti. 4:2 to be prepared in season and out of season. We never know in advance when an emergency will arise. Being prepared will enable us to deal with the problem with greater confidence.

How much money do you need in such a fund? Consider your lifestyle and determine from your budget how much it would cost to meet all your obligations during an average month. Having determined this, you need to decide how many months reserve you would like to accumulate. Remember the story of Joseph, how he was to store up his grain so that he would have enough in the lean years. Following the example set for us by Joseph, having an emergency fund is wise.

With a fund in place, an unexpected death, accident, loss of a job or perhaps the opportunity of a lifetime, need not place a stress on your finances. Whatever the situation, extra funds set aside through planning will prevent unnecessary stress.

Place one family member in charge of the fund and have them report regularly on its growth, including the amount of interest you have earned.

An emergency fund can be built into your budget and accumulate over a period of time. It should not in itself become a source of stress. Remember that this money is set aside for emergencies and is not a source of ready cash to pay for new golf clubs or a vacation.

By completing the following chart, you can determine how must money to set aside in an emergency fund.

Monthly income required to meet obligations	$_____
Amount required X _____ months required	$_____
Divide the amount required by twelve months to see how much you need to save every month	$_____

Include this amount in your monthly budget and deposit the money into a separate account. It would be wise to have a joint account with one person managing the account. The Bible teaches us that even the ant "prepares her food in the summer, and gathers her provision in the harvest." (Pr. 6:8)

On The Road to Debt Free Living

5

In September 1989, I met a lady in Vancouver who cheerfully told me that she and her husband were now debt free. I was certainly pleased to learn that this couple had followed the suggestions in my book "What Every Christian Should Know About Money Management."

Applying basic principles to their financial situation, they were debt free in eight short months. They are a rare couple who stand as living proof that debt free living is possible. Let no debt remain outstanding, (Ro. 13:8) and if need be "go sell your oil and pay your debt" (2Ki:4:7.) If you are facing a debt situation and are serious about becoming debt free, consider reading the above mentioned book and apply the following suggestions:

1. Stop using credit cards.

2. Prepare a budget and give all family members an opportunity to participate in establishing the budget.

3. Pay off the debt with the highest interest rate first.

4. Return items which were just purchased and not needed.

5. Consider seeking professional help from a non-profit credit counselling service. A credit counsellor will assess your situation and help establish a supervised payment program. Normally, the initial visit is free

and then you are charged according to your ability to pay. Many municipalities across Canada offer this service.

6. Stay in touch with your creditors. Let them know you have made a plan to eliminate your debt and ask for their help. They may even stop the interest clock if you were to ask. I know some creditors who have settled for a reduced amount, if the indebtedness was paid at once.

7. Be careful about a debt-consolidation loan. At first this may sound great, but if you are not well disciplined you may end up in a worse situation than when you began. Experience has shown me that when the monthly payment is reduced and the cash flow increases, people tend to think they are debt free.

The danger lies in the attitude that you can now make a small purchase on your credit card. After all, you have more money available each month and can handle your payments without any problems. Before long, the credit card is topped up again and you need another consolidation loan. When will the spiral stop? Remember, debt consolidation is a bandage approach.

The answer is, your attitude and your lifestyle may need to change, assuming you seriously want to be debt-free.

Debt Avoidance

Avoid incurring debt. Consider what was said in Matthew 18:25, "Since he was not able to pay, the master ordered that he and his wife and his children and all that he had be sold to repay the debt." Debt is subtle in that it can slowly and sometimes quickly erase all that you have acquired. Never be casual with debt because it will always be ruthless with you.

If you want to avoid getting into debt, you must learn to recognize the danger signs. Some of the danger signs include: making minimum payments on your credit cards, considering a debt consolidation loan, not being able to pay your tithe or save any money.

Here are some suggestions to help you get out of debt while avoiding further liabilities.

1. Commit yourself to seeking God's help. We frequently cheat God by not giving Him a chance to supply our needs. When we depend on credit cards, we eliminate God from the process. Had we been patient, He might have led us to a sale price for the item we wanted or convinced us that we didn't need the item in the first place.

2. Do not carry credit cards or a check book when you are shopping. Use cash and shop around for the best prices.

3. Avoid impulse buying. Most impulse buying is based on emotion and results in the purchase of poor quality, over-priced merchandise.

4. You are a steward of the funds entrusted to your care. In the book of Luke, we read that we will all be held accountable for our stewardship. For the present, be accountable to your spouse for each expenditure you make. If it can't clearly be justified, and you have already made the purchase, return it for a refund.

5. Determine to buy only sale merchandise. Consider the percentage savings and not only the dollar amount. If I were to tell you where to receive twenty percent interest on your investments, you would be interested. Look at items you need in the same light. When using a credit card the price of items purchased increases by the interest charges. With some credit cards, this can be a substantial increase in the cost of items purchased. Currently, most credit card issuers are charging over twenty pecent interest.

6. Commit your plans to God. Pray for wisdom and guidance in your financial situation. God answers prayer if we are praying with the correct motive. Be prepared to fight temptation, just as Jesus did in the desert. (1Co:10:13)

7. Decide to avoid credit card debt in the future.

This is a good time for all Christians to become debt-free. You do not need to be an economist to recognize Canada's economic problems. Higher interest rates, increasing inflation, higher taxes, major national debt, and a slowing of our economy, are all warning signs.

We must establish financial goals and follow a financial plan. However, the biggest danger we face is procrastination. You may decide to put your financial plan in place next month, after you receive that anticipated raise. The increase fails to materialize and another month goes by. The time you have lost without a financial plan means interest charges on your credit cards have put you further into debt.

Procrastination is not one of the problems, it is the problem. NOW is the time to get out of debt.

Credit Cards (And You)

6

The Danger In Credit Cards

Credit cards can be dangerous! A clear message is given us in Proverbs 7:22 where the Bible states, "the borrower is servant to the lender." When using a credit card we are in fact borrowing from the owner, the credit card company. Since more credit card users are paying the balance of their account each month, credit card companies are beginning to charge an annual or usage fee for the card.

Even if you are one of the people who pays your credit card each month, you spend more money and are tempted by impulse buying with a credit card.

At your finger tips, a credit card when used incorrectly, will

- charge you maximum interest,

- entice you to spend more money than you can afford,

- cause family stress,

- allow you to spend beyond your limit,

- persuade you to buy on impulse,

- make you a servant of the lender,

- promise you the good life but never really deliver, and

- put you into debt.

Credit cards are quite easy to obtain because credit card companies, banks, trust companies and retailers make huge profits from users. Not only are credit cards abused, however, they are a tempting target for thieves.

Ironically, if our wallet was stolen, we would probably look to see if any cash was missing before counting our credit cards. Credit card theft, however, is big business. Many thieves not only steal your card and use it, some even return the card to your wallet or purse before you realize it is missing. At the end of the month you get the bill and now must persuade a credit card company that you didn't make the purchase.

When you do not have the cash to pay for that dress or set of golf clubs you have always wanted, it's rather painless to use a plastic card. After all, the minimum payment you make next month is much less than the purchase price. You fool yourself into thinking that because you can make a minimum payment, one more purchase will not affect your cash flow. Soon all those little purchases can add up to unmanageable debt.

Debt management is the ability to control your debt instead of your debt controlling you. Too many people think poor debt management can't happen to them. I have met individuals with incomes of $100,000 who are bogged down in financial problems. They don't know where or how to start drawing up a budget and have totally lost control of their finances.

The problem with using credit cards and making only minimum payments, is that interest charges soon soar out of control. Note the slope of the curve in the graph below. This graph plots the life of a credit card on which no payments have been made for two years.

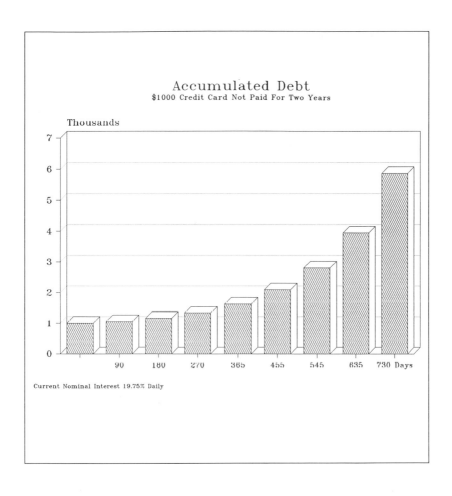

Accumulated Debt
$1000 Credit Card Not Paid For Two Years

Thousands

Current Nominal Interest 19.75% Daily

I realize that most of us pay off our credit cards on a regular basis. We are warned of this in the book of John where we read "The thief comes only to steal, kill and destroy." For many, that is exactly what has occurred. The credit thief has stolen their dignity, killed their will, excitement, joy, adventure, fun, their hope and finally their spirit.

But, there is hope! The verse goes on to say "I (Jesus speaking) have come that they may have life, and have it to the full'. (Jn. 10:10) Regardless of the size of your debt, God is Bigger! "For nothing is impossible with God." (Lk. 1:37) "in all things God works for the good of those who love Him, who have been called according to His purpose." (Rm:8,28)

Controlling
(Credit Cards)

7

Credit cards are frequently used for impulse buying. This type of shopping will lead to trouble. Be careful not to use credit cards for things which will be abandoned before you have paid for them as this would be wasteful. It was the Lord who set the example for us when He instructed His disciples to "Gather the pieces that are left over. Let nothing be wasted."(Jn.6:12)

If you have made regular payments, the credit card company will often increase your limit without even notifying you. Your limit is usually printed on your monthly statement.

Banks, retailers and other credit card issuers make a huge profit on the interest charges associated with credit cards. They also supplement their income through charging user fees for their credit cards.

Interest rates on credit cards vary. Do you know the current interest rates on the cards you carry? Do you know if the interest is calculated at the time you make your purchase or when the transaction is posted? If you make a partial payment, the interest is sometimes calculated on the full amount prior to your payment.

Be cautious about using credit cards. It is easy to get into debt and very difficult to remove the debt. Debt places a heavy strain on marriage relationships and is one of the leading causes of marriage breakdown.

Credit cards in themselves are not bad, it is just so easy to abuse them. When I was a frequent user of credit cards, my wife, Donna, challenged me to go through the summer without using any credit cards. I told her it would be no problem, but secretly, I did not know how I would last two months. I placed the cards into a drawer and promptly forgot about them. Late in the fall, I realized I did not need the cards and destroyed them. They melt well at 350 degrees or you can create wonderful designs with a credit card and scissors.

How To Use Credit Cards!

- Do not carry a credit card.

- Plan your purchases in advance. Find the item you need, preferably on sale and return home to get your card. I know it is inconvenient, but you get a chance to think about your purchase without sales pressure.

- If you cannot pay your credit card in full each month, stop using the card.

- Set limits on purchases. Anything beyond a certain dollar amount requires spousal approval.

- Determine to only buy items which are on sale.

- Only one credit card for the family.

- Prepare a family budget. Use the forms found in the back of this book.

You probably feel you are able to handle credit cards fairly well. Remember, even when you do pay the full balance every month, you still spend more money than if you had used cash or cheques.

The following is a brief quiz to help gain a perspective on credit card usage. Answer the following questions either True or False.

Credit Card Useage Quiz

1.	I use my credit card every week	T	F
2.	I pay the full amount each month	T	F
3.	I make minimum payments each month	T	F
4.	I have more than one similar card	T	F
5.	I currently have no credit card debt	T	F
6.	I exceed my credit card limit	T	F
7.	I do not keep credit card receipts	T	F
8.	I have used my credit card for cash advances	T	F
9.	I am surprised by the amount of my bill	T	F
10.	I have missed a monthly payment	T	F
11.	I cry myself to sleep	T	F
12.	I have been asked to return my card	T	F

Breaking The Credit Card Cycle

8

Breaking Free

If you are serious about resolving credit card debt, the following suggestions are a good place to start. You might also wish to add some ideas that are specific to your own situation. Before you begin following any of the following suggestions, be sure to commit yourself to prayer and ask the Lord to help you. "I sought the Lord, and he answered me; he delivered me from all my fears."(Ps.34:4) In the same passage we read further where it is proclaimed; "This poor man called, and the Lord heard him; he saved him out of all his troubles."(Ps.34:6)

1. Return all credit cards to the issuer. Be sure you cut the cards in half before mailing them back.

2. With the credit cards, enclose a letter requesting that your account be closed. Have each party sign the letter.

3. Make a listing of all credit card debt and the interest rate being charged. Be sure to note the frequency of interest calculation. The more often the calculation, the more money you will pay.

4. Prepare a schedule of credit card repayment indicating outstanding amount, interest charges, minimum payment required and the amount of your intended payment.

5. Prepare a budget and allocate money to pay off the credit card debt, beginning with the cards which charge the highest interest.

6. Have all participants involved in the budgeting process make a verbal and written commitment to follow thc budgot.

7. Review your progress together at regular intervals.

8. Appoint one person to keep track of the debt reduction and report to the group. Alternate this responsibility on a regular basis.

9. Do not re-apply for a credit card when the debt has been fully paid.

Bankruptcy Is No Option

9

Bankruptcy

Bankruptcy is not necessarily an option available to a Christian facing serious financial difficulties. This may sound harsh, but, we usually end up in this situation because we have not applied discipline and God's principles to the way we handle money.

Bankruptcy is a bandage approach to solving a much deeper problem. It only allows us to run away from our responsibilities without getting to the root of the difficulty. We are called to be separate from the way the world operates, so I feel we have a moral responsibility to pay our debts. Let no debt remain outstanding, (Ro. 13:8) and if need be "go sell your oil and pay your debt."(2Ki.4:7)

For the most part, bankruptcy can be avoided. Bankruptcy is sometimes the end result of poor money management, or generally bad management of either a business or personal situation. There are a number of agencies which will help us avoid this problem or we should see an accountant or financial planner at the first sign of difficulty. Instead, we often wait until we are so deeply into debt that the road back is long and difficult. Early detection of financial problems is important.

As Christians, we are called to be wise. If we lack wisdom, James calls upon us to seek wisdom from God in all situations.(Ja.1:5) We have a moral obligation to resolve our debt and God can give us wisdom in this situation.

If your debt is mounting and you need help, consider some of the following steps to solve your dilemma.

1. Bankruptcy is an easy way out, and no option for a Christian.

2. Speak to your creditors early and ask for their help. Be sure to stress your intention to honour your financial commitment. (Mt.5:25)

3. Request that they stop charging you interest on the debt and agree to an affordable payment plan until the debt is paid in full.(Mt.5:25)

4. Prepare a budget and review your circumstances with a professional financial counsellor. (Pr.11:14)

5. Avoid purchases or situations that would increase your indebtedness. (Lk.14:28)

6. Examine where you can cut back on your expenditures.

7. Determine which depreciating items you could sell, applying the proceeds to your debt.

Goals ...
Who Needs Them?

10

The story is told about a man who was asked what his goal was in life. "Well," he said. "I get up in the morning, go to work, come home, watch television and then go to bed."

"What do you do the next day," he was asked. "Well, I get up in the morning, go to work, come home, watch television, go to bed and then get up the next morning, go to work..."

This describes many of our lives. Without goals, life can become a meaningless blur and before we know, it's all over. We might have dreams of doing things with our life. We might have dreams of becoming financially secure, some day. But, unless we set goals, our dreams will remain just that.. Dreams.

Most Canadians do not have any written goals. Without goals, it's difficult to know where you are going in life. The Apostle Paul spoke of having a goal when he said, "I press on toward the goal to win the prize for which God has called me heavenward in Christ Jesus."(Php.3:14)

Goals are your measuring stick, or a progress barometer. To become reality, goals need to be flexible, measurable, obtainable, specific and realistic. Procrastination is the reason most of us do not have any specific goals. We just do not take the time to sit down, discuss and plan our lives. Ironically, we are frequently required to submit goals to our employers and we do it willingly and quickly. Successful people make a plan and work their plan. Perhaps today is the time to begin focusing on your goals.

Divide your goals into two groups. The first group will meet your short term needs. These are goals which you usually accomplish in less than a year. By contrast, long term goals are those which usually take more than a year to accomplish.

Goals require a commitment. Goals seldom get completed without a commitment to reach them. Few success stories occur on their own. Success demands goals. Set up regular review dates because your goals may need to be changed at certain points in life.

Goals need to be discussed between both spouses and, in some circumstances, children should be included in the process. Goals need agreement among all family members and should become a prayer priority. "Commit to the Lord whatever you do, and your plan will succeed."(Pr.16:3)The commands given to Joshua still are valid today as when received by him, "Do not let this Book of the Law depart from your mouth; meditate on it day and night, so that you may be careful to do everything written in it. Then you will be prosperous and successful."(Jos.1:8)

Use the following form to set your goals.

Goals

Short Term	1. _____
	2. _____
	3. _____
Long Term	1. _____
	2. _____
	3. _____
Review Date	_____

If your goals are financial goals, they should meet your family's immediate need for financial security. Regardless of the reasons for wanting to make changes in your financial situation, you must set clear, concrete goals. Your goals must be sensible and take into consideration your lifestyle.

Winners Keep On Running

11

Never give up regardless of how desperate your financial situation may be! God is able to do all that He has promised. Consider Eph.3:20 " Now to IIim who is able to do immeasurably more than all we ask or imagine, according to his power that is at work within us."

Financial success depends on us establishing correct priorities. These priorities must be set by discovering what God wants us to do with our finances. One thing God wants for Christians is that they not be indebted to other people. "Let no debt remain outstanding, except the continuing debt to love one another." (Rom. 13:8)

The first step to financial success is to prepare a family budget and make plans for paying off all your debts. Once this is in place and a debt repayment plan has been established, you are moving towards financial freedom.

Your attitude plays an important part at this stage. Winners have a winning attitude. They face the challenge knowing that "greater is He that is in you than He that is in the world." Regardless of how desperate your situation may be, your attitude must be positive as you realize that God wants you to be debt free and He will help you.

Those who acquire a debt free lifestyle should then help other Christians attain the same position so they can also escape the tensions indebtedness can cause. The second step on the road to financial freedom is to persevere, persevere and persevere.

After considering the following illustration, would you persevere if you were in this situation?

- Born into a poor family
- Had a demanding childhood
- Less than a year of formal education
- Failed in business, 1831
- Defeated in race for legislature, 1832
- Failed in business again, 1833
- Elected to legislature, 1834
- Fiancee dies, 1835
- Defeated in election as Speaker, 1838
- Defeated in election, 1840
- Enters into an unhappy marriage, 1842
- Three of four children die before age 18
- Defeated in election to Congress, 1843
- Elected to Congress, 1846
- Defeated in election to Congress, 1848
- Defeated in election to Senate, 1855
- Defeated in attempt to become Vice-President, 1856
- Defeated in election to Senate, 1858
- Elected President, 1860
- Died a few days after ending the civil war

Abraham Lincoln, was a man who didn't understand the meaning of the words "give up." By any standard of measurement he was a winner.

Perseverance produces character; and character produces hope. Hope does not disappoint us, because God has poured out his love into our hearts by the Holy Spirit, whom he has given us."(Ro.5:4,5)We are able to keep on persevering because "the one who is in us is greater than the one who is in the world."(1Jo.4:4)

Buying A Car

12

After discussing debt, credit cards this seems a good time to discuss spending money wisely, i.e. buying a car.

For me, buying a car has usually been a painful experience. Each purchase has offered lessons in handling arrogance, promises which disappear when you drive off the lot, insults and in some cases rudeness. In Rev. John C. Maxwell's book Your Attitude, Key To Success, he relates a story that points out the following when discussing why customers quit. He states that 68% quit because of an attitude of indifference toward them by some employee.

In the auto industry the salesperson's behaviour is often aimed at gaining control of the situation. They try to identify the type of buyer you are and then proceed to let you know they are in charge. Of course, there are exceptions to every rule, but my own experiences have not been the exception.

To be successful in any enterprise, we need to follow the example Jesus set. We need to acquire a servants' attitude. When we put the other person ahead of our own interests, we are true to scripture and the relationship will, in most cases, be beneficial to all parties. This should apply to Christian salespeople and buyers. As salespeople are just as quick to point out, many buyers can also be quite arrogant, insulting and rude.

Once you have found a salesperson that treats you with respect, what should you consider when buying a new or used car?

Buying a New Car

1. Decide on the size of car you want to purchase. Should it be subcompact, compact, mid-size or full-size? Research the car you want to buy before visiting the dealership. Read reports on the various automobiles in Consumers Report Magazine or contact the Canadian Automotive Association, Automotive Protection Association and other reliable sources. Visit your local bookstore and purchase The Lemon-Aid New Car Guide and the Auto Guide.

2. Decide on any options you want on the car, before you visit the showroom. Sales people play on your emotions and may try to work spouses against each other. Be sure you are familiar with all warranties and the servicing required to validate any warranty.

3. Consider how you will finance this car. Shop around for the best interest rates. Compare banks, trusts companies, credit unions, private funding and dealership rates. Whoever finances your car is making a sizable amount of money so be sure your contract is open. An open contract allows for prepayment to settle or reduce the account at any time. Read the entire contract before signing anything.

4. Decide what you can afford to pay for a car, including your finance charges, and walk out of the dealership if the price is too high or the dealer is not willing to meet your offer. There will always be another "good deal" elsewhere.

5. Be sure to test drive the car. If possible, test drive an older model of the car you are considering. This will give you some idea of how the car will feel two or three years from now.

6. When you finally decide on which car to buy and have agreed to a price, the dealership will try to increase the size of the sale by offering special packages. They will talk about rust proofing, extended maintenance, special finishes and other items. These

are added onto the final price of the car and are usually subject to financing. These things may be beneficial but can be very expensive if you finance them.

Decisions in Buying A Used Car

There are two ways to buy a used car. One option is a dealership and the second is a private sale. When buying a used car, we tend to focus on the price rather than its mileage and mechanical condition. Most people are not knowledgeable about the mechanical aspects of cars and rely mainly on a car's eye appeal.

Buying a used car can be a mixed experience. If you are familiar and knowledgeable about cars you will often do quite well with your purchase. If your mechanical knowledge of cars is limited to pumping your own gas, you will need to do some homework to avoid buying someone else's problem.

Purchasing a used car can be time consuming, but you should avoid making quick decisions. Once you decide on the make and model of car you want, there are a number of points to consider.

A Few Items To Look For In A Good Used Car

- Is it Affordable
- Low mileage
- Even wear on tires
- No body rust or ripples in the car body
- Discolouration
- Regular maintenance and servicing
- Clean exhaust
- Easy to start and smooth idle

Before agreeing to purchase the car, you should take it to a reliable mechanic for his assessment of its mechanical fitness. Book stores and libraries are a good source of books and magazines to assist you in purchasing a used car.

Buying A House "Caveat Emptor"

13

For most of us, a house purchase is our biggest investment. If you do not do your homework, it could also become one of your biggest headaches. As any other purchase, it is advisable to take some time and investigate before you invest.

Here are a few suggestions to consider before signing on the dotted line.

1. Arrange for a pre-approved mortgage. Be sure to shop around for your mortgage, since rates vary among lenders.

2. There are several types of mortgages available. Be sure you understand all the conditions and terms involved. Investigate thoroughly and you could save thousands of dollars.

3. When you find your dream home, check with the municipal office for: fire access, churches, shopping, parks, commuting ease, schools and future traffic patterns. You could spend 30 minutes each day walking your child to school or, wake up some morning and find an expressway running past your front door.

4. Investigate the builder. Ask a former purchaser about the quality of workmanship, after sales service, and flexibility.

5. NEVER SIGN AN OFFER TO PURCHASE BEFORE YOUR LAWYER HAS REVIEWED THE DOCUMENT! Normally, you cannot make changes in your offer to purchase after it has been signed.

6. If it is a new house, be sure to include any changes to the house, and conditions outlined by the builder in the offer to purchase agreement. The builder may be planting a juniper bush in your front yard. Of course, this is the one plant you are allergic too.

7. Prepare in advance for the closing costs. Ask your lawyer what he will charge to handle the paperwork for the sale of your old property (if you have one) and his services on your new property. Ask for an estimate of any Land Transfer Taxes and other related closing costs. Don't forget adjustments for prepaid taxes, heating fuel, hydro, cable television, telephone and any other expenses the vendor may have paid.

8. Be careful to select an appropriate closing date for this transaction. Moving expenses are less in the middle of the week and before month end. Your lawyer will also thank you. He will have a much easier time at the registry office if the closing date is during the week and not at the end of the month.

Remember ....

Never sign an offer to purchase before your lawyer has reviewed the document.

How to Buy Your First House

14

How To Buy Your First Home

Historically, owning a home in Canada has been a wise investment for many Canadians. Besides ensuring a source of income during the retirement years, home ownership can provide years of pleasure and memories for most families. Today, however, home ownership is only a dream for many Canadians who are often discouraged that they can't afford a place twice as large as their parents' first home.

We live in a society where marketing agencies seek to convince us that we need everything immediately. The bigger, brighter or cleaner the product the better. The scriptures, however, teach us "to be still and know that I am God." (Ps. 46:10) If we listen to the persuasive marketing schemes, we tend to exclude God from our daily lives and make our financial plans without consulting Him. Both Matthew and Luke remind us to "Seek first the kingdom of God, and His righteousness, and all these things will be given you as well."

When it comes to home ownership or any other decision in our lives, this passage teaches us two important principals. The first part talks about our obligation to seek God and His righteousness. Clearly, God is to come first in our life. Secondly, in seeking God and His righteousness, God will ensure that our needs are met.

Most people desire the so called "good life" because it acts as a barometer to measure success. This "good life," fed by advertising, does not allow us to consider second best. In the area of home ownership, few seem satisfied with the "starter home" which may require some repair or is much smaller than we would like.

Perhaps the following suggestions will serve as a guideline for those individuals desiring to purchase their first home without getting into unmanageable debt.

1. Pray and ask God's help and guidance in selecting the house He would want for you. Proverbs 16:3 tells us to commit our plans to the Lord and they will succeed.

2. Be realistic in your expectations. You want to enter the housing market, but, you do not need the biggest and most expensive house.

3. Consider moving out of a city or town and commute to work. Houses in smaller villages, towns or rural areas tend to cost less and offer more amenities.

4. Evaluate housing alternatives. Examine condominiums, townhouses, semi-detached and detached housing. Your first home will probably not be your last.

5. If you have depreciating assets such as a motorcycle or a boat, sell them and use the money as part of your downpayment.

6. Consider a joint-ownership or partnership with a family member. Perhaps someone in your family would provide the downpayment, (or part of the downpayment) for a percentage share in the future equity growth. This could be appealing as an investment, (allows the investor to utilize some of their capital gains exemption) and helpful to you.

7. A family member may be willing to provide an interest free mortgage or second mortgage on the home for a short period of time. This means all your monthly payments would be applied directly to the outstanding principal.

The lender helps you buy your first home and each month's payment received from you would provide regular monthly income. Also, since this is an interest free loan, the monthly payment received from you is non-taxable since it is their money being returned to them.

If you had money in a saving account earning 12 percent interest, it is subject to inflation and you must pay taxes on interest earned. The effect of allowing for 5 percent inflation and a marginal tax rate of 40% is as follows:

Rate of Return before taxes	12%
Less	
Taxes @ 40% = 4.8	
Inflation 5%	
	9.8%
Real Rate of Return adjusted for inflation	2.2%

The difference between helping a family member buy their first home or earning interest on your money is 2.2%. We are all aware of the parable of the talents and that we are required to get a return on our investments, consider the investment in your family as ordained by God in the second chapter of Genesis.

8. Discuss and determine joint goals for you and your spouse. Having a goal is critical to achieving anything in life. President John F. Kennedy gave America the goal to put a man on the moon by the end of the decade. In itself, there is nothing spectacular about setting a goal.

    What is interesting about this goal, is that it was technologically impossible to accomplish the goal at that time. Obviously the nation responded to the challenge and reached the goal within a decade.

9. Consider various options. Move from your city or province if you must. Consider part-time work. If you are saving money until you have the downpayment, compare your savings with the increasing house prices in the particular area you want to live.

Assume you can put aside $100 or $250 a month towards the purchase of a home. At the end of one year you save between $1200 and $1800, plus interest earned on your money. Depending on the type of account and frequency of interest calculation, you could earn approximately $200 in taxable income.

Interest Earned	$200.00
Less	
Taxes (marginal rate 39%) $78.00	
Inflation Rate at 5% $10.00	
Net Return	$112.00

The average house price in Metropolitan Toronto was around $277,000 in September 1989. Lets assume we find a nice starter house for $150,000. A five percent increase in the price of the home would increase it's cost by $7,500.

This might put the house out of reach for many people who are relying on savings to purchase their home. Their savings are often less per year than the yearly increase in home prices. For this reason you

Source: Average House Price In Metro Toronto 1989 Royal
Lepage, Survey of Canadian House Prices

must be creative in your thinking when it comes to buying your first home.

Once your decide to buy a house, your anxiety doesn't end there. (Even though the Scriptures tell us not to worry, too often we still do.) I well remember the day I bought my first home. I walked the floor most of the night and when I finally went to bed I was unable to sleep. This routine lasted for about 4 nights.

I was suffering from that common disease known as "buyer's remorse." On several occasions I wanted to cancel the agreement to purchase and put an end to all the worry. Years later, of course, I realized that buying the house turned out to be a very wise investment. I'm certainly glad I didn't change my mind.

We can see a principle in the Old Testament which puts the whole matter in a clearer perspective. Remember how Moses sent out 12 spies to investigate the promised land? Their mission was to report on what they saw and whether they could conquer the land. When they returned, 10 spies said victory was impossible. The inhabitants where bigger, stronger and could easily turn back God's people.

The other two spies, Caleb and Joshua, were just as convinced that the people could conquer the land. They must have felt tremendous pressure from the other ten to change their verdict so that they could return to Moses with a unanimous verdict. Caleb and Joshua refused to change their belief. They persevered, put the Lord first, and went after their goal.

Moses now had a problem. Who could he believe? All of the spies saw the same thing, went into the same land but came back with two very different decisions.

Are you familiar with the eighty/twenty rule? It argues that eighty percent of your success will come from twenty percent of your decisions or sales. Caleb and Joshua exemplify the eighty/twenty rule. Approximately eighty percent of the spies said they could not be successful and twenty percent said they would be successful.

If you are going to buy your first home, your attitude or perseverance, will likely make the difference between success or failure. When the odds of your decision to buy a house are four to one against you, remember Caleb and Joshua.

Calculating The Cost

15

Calculating Your Cost For A New Home

When we move into a new home they have a lot more to consider than the colour of their drapes or size of the lawn. In calculating how much it will cost to move into our new home, we must take into account the following:

a) Price of the home and the operating costs. Complete the following new home budget. Use schedules 1, 2 and 3. You now have a clear picture of the finances you need to move into your new home.

b) The expenses we will pay at the time of closing. Determine our closing expenses by completing schedules 4,5 and 6.

c) We must also consider total family income to determine if we can manage the monthly payments.

d) By using the following schedules you will get a clear picture of your finances in light of your decision to buy a house.

Schedule 1

Purchase price of the home $ _____

Less

Available downpayment $ _____

Proposed mortgage amount $ _____

Schedule 2

Proposed monthly mortgage $ _____

Proposed monthly taxes $ _____

Total monthly payment $ _____

Schedule 3

New Home Operating Expenses

Monthly Mortgage $ _____

Property Taxes $ _____

Condominium Fees $ _____

Utilities (Water, Hydro) $ _____

Heating Costs $ _____

Communications (Phone, Cable) $ _____

Property Insurance $ _____

Appliances $ _____

Repairs/Renovations $ _____

Tools (Lawn Mower, Shovels) $ _____

Other $ _____

Total Monthly Expenses $

Schedule 4

Available Cash

Money In Savings $ _____

Canada Savings Bonds $ _____

Canadian Securities $ _____

Residue From Sale Of House $ _____

Miscellaneous $ _____

Other $ _____

Total Cash Available $

Schedule 5

Moving Expenses

Moving Company	$ _____
Utility Deposits (Phone Hydro)	$
Moving Equipment	$ _____
Packing Material	$ _____
Storage Costs	$ _____
Temporary Lodging	$ _____
Other	$ _____
Total Moving Expenses	$

Schedule 6

Closing Expenses

Lawyer's Fees	$ _____
Mortgage Fees	$ _____
Land Transfer Tax	$ _____
Adjustments (Fuel, Prepaid Taxes)	$ _____
Registration Fees	$ _____
Appraisal Fees	$ _____
Proposed GST	$ _____
Total Closing Costs	$

Share The Investment

16

Sharing The Investment

Sharing is a biblical principal. When a Christian shares with others he is honouring God. "Because of the service by which you have proved yourselves, men will praise God for the obedience that accompanies your confession of the gospel of Christ, and for your generosity in sharing with them and with everyone else." (2Co.9:13) It would appear that we face a test when it comes to sharing with others. If we are obedient, then God receives the glory. In Lk. 3:11 the apostle John says," The man with two tunics should share with him who has none, and the one who has food should do the same."

With house prices soaring out of reach for many people, this type of arrangement would allow more people to enter the housing market. Under this arrangement, a family member or close friend would invest in your new house as a partner. You would provide part of the down payment while your partner provides the remaining money.

Each party would share in the proceeds from the final sale of the property in a ratio agreed to at the outset. Whatever arrangement is made between you and say, Aunt Loaded, be sure it is in writing, signed and witnessed.

Assume you and your favourite Aunt Loaded buy a home for $200,000. The down payment required is $50,000.00. If the house increased in value at the rate of eight percent each year, and you both agreed to sell the house in five years, you would have a substantial gain.

Purchase Price	$200,000.00	
Downpayment		
Your Share	$ 37,500.00	
Aunt Loaded	$ 12,500.00	
Remaining Mortgage		$150,000.00
House Value In Five Years		
Selling Price	$293,900.00	
Less Fees	$ 17,700.00	
Net From Sale	$277,300.00	
Less:		
Outstanding Mortgage	$200,000.00	
Profit		$77,300.00

Each partner would receive their original investment plus interese as follows:

Your return	$57,975.00
Aunt Loaded	$19,325.00

You are now in a position to look for another house without the help of Aunt Loaded.

If you decide not to sell the house at the end of five years, you could have its value appraised and use this figure as the potential selling price. You could then arrange a second mortgage on the house and use the proceeds to pay Aunt Loaded. Your benefit during the five years has been a place to live while building up equity in a home.

This type of arrangement can be completely flexible. For example, you could pay the loan from Aunt Loaded during a five year period at a specified rate of interest instead of sharing the profit after five years.

Reducing The Interest Rate On Mortgages

Canada Trust recently introduced a mortgage to allow parents to help their children own a home. The plan works as follows: the parent places minimum $20,000 into a GIC with Canada Trust and requests a lower than posted rate of return on the GIC. If the GIC rate was 12.5%, the parent could opt to receive 8%, or any other amount they determine.

Canada Trust will apply the same rate reduction to the mortgage of the children, for the same amount and term selected above. This means the kids would have a lower rated mortgage increasing their cash flow.

The smallest amount is $20,000 but, it could be for the full amount of the mortgage, if the parents had the money. You can choose any term from one to five years. The GIC isn't held as collateral and Canada Trust accepts full risk for repayment of the mortgage by the kids. You do not co-sign the mortgage. (Pr.11/15)

The parents will pay less income tax, since they receive less interest income, and the children will not be required to pay tax on the benefit they receive. In effect, it is another way to split income with your children.

It's A Paradox **17**

It's A Paradox

When we examine the way the world operates and compare it to various biblical principals, we discover conflicting values. The following are some of the obvious differences.

World	Biblical
The one with the most toys wins	Put no hope in wealth (1Ti.6:17)
Go for broke and risk it all	Plan for success (Pr.16:3)
Desires instant gratification of wants	Wait and depend upon the Lord (P.46:10)
Loves money and uses it to prove success	Love of money corrupts (1Ti.6:17)
Lend money at maximum interest	Do not charge your Christian brother interest on a loan (Ex.22:25)
Rely on get-rich-quick ideas	Plan for success and seek many advisors (Pr.15:22;20:18)
Hire at minimum wage	A man is worthy of his hire (Lk. 10:7)
Do only what is necessary to get by	Excellence is rewarded by standing before kings. (Pr. 22:29)
I deserve a break	Focus on God and seek His kingdom (Mt. 6:33)

World	Biblical
Charity begins at home	Give to him who asks (Mt. 5:42)
Rules with authoritarian manner	Consider others better than yourself (Lev. 25:53)
Work to please your boss	Work as unto the Lord (Col. 3:23)
Promise anything, just get the job done	Honour your vows as before the Lord (Dt. 23:21)
Bankruptcy ends a multitude of problems	Perseverance builds character and a man's reputation is worth more than gold or silver (Ro.5:3,4)
Outward appearance and keeping up with the Joneses is important	Christians are not to covet their neighbour's possessions (Ex. 20:17)
Act as a co-signor on a loan	Do not co-sign for any loan (Pr.11:15)
Hang onto wealth with a firm grasp	Give and it will be given you (Lk.6:38)
Bequest everything to your children or to others when you die	Honour the Lord from your wealth AND first fruits (Pr.3:9,10)
False reporting on taxes is acceptable	Render to Caesar what is Caesar's and to God what is God's (Mt.22:21)
Strive for material gain	Humility and fear of the Lord bring wealth, honour and life (Pr.22:4)
The poor deserve their situation	How blessed is he who considers the helpless; the Lord will deliver him in a day of trouble (Ps.41:1)
Procrastinate: plan later, when it is necessary	Commit your plans to the Lord then they will succeed. (Pr.16:3)
Hard work is for suckers, let the other guy do it	The hand of the diligent makes rich. (Pr.10:4)
Worry about wealth, making it and keeping it	Cast all your cares on Him, because He cares for you (1Pt 5:7)
Do not prepare for retirement	Ants are creatures of little power, yet they store up their food in the summer (Pr. 30:25)
Conform to the acceptable practices of the world	Be separate from the world (Rm. 12:1)

Banks and Trust Companies: Like Mortgages

18

You have decided to buy a house. After weeks of planning, going over your finances with a fine tooth comb and studying the housing market, you are now sitting nervously in the bank applying for a mortgage.

You and your wife exchange bewildering glances as the mortgage officer devours your financial statement. The only sound is your heartbeat and the loan officer's adding machine. Every so often he grunts and peeks over his glasses at your anxious faces.

After what seems like an hour (it was only 15 minutes), he lifts his head, smiles and sticks out his hand. Congratulations he says, we will provide you with a mortgage. As you float out of his office, it feels as if you have just inherited a fortune. In fact, over the next 25 years, the real winner may not be you. The bank is the one who has just inherited a fortune. Yours!

Lets say you have just taken out a $70,000 mortgage at 12%. You will pay off this loan over 25 years. At the end of 25 years however, your $70,000 loan will cost you $216,698.34. Of this amount, $146,698.34 goes toward interest charges. And you thought the bank was doing you a favour!

There is still a chance for you to cut your losses while decreasing the bank's profit margin on your home. Following are just some of the methods you can use.

1. Pay extra money on your mortgage every year

You can do this if you hold a mortgage that allows you to pay an extra amount of money each year or perhaps every month. This amount is applied directly towards the principal and can save you thousands of dollars in interest charges. Normally, you will find a repayment provision for ten or fifteen percent of your mortgage on the anniversary date. It is amazing how much money you will save in payments that will not be made in the future because your mortgage is paid off sooner.

2. Change your amortization period from 25 to 20 years

Banks and trust companies will automatically assume you will pay your mortgage off in 25 years. If you ask for an amortization period of 20 years, your monthly payment on our example $70,000 mortgage will increase from $722.33 per month to $756.68. The $34.35 different in monthly payments will save you $45,093.51 in interest payments over the life of the mortgage. This is an exorbitant savings considering you are only paying an extra $1.15 per day. This would not even buy you a cup of coffee and a donut in most coffee shops.

3. Make weekly payments instead of monthly payments

If you made weekly payments instead of monthly payments, you would be making one extra payment each year. At the same time, your house would than be paid for in 18 years instead of 25 years. If you decide on a weekly payment schedule, make sure you are able to switch back to monthly payments if you find your budget is too tight. Lenders sometimes ask for a fee when switching from one type of mortgage to another, so be sure to get all the details before you sign on the dotted line.

4. Make Cash Deposits Against The Principal

Combine the idea mentioned in our first point with a weekly or bi-weekly payment program and you will reduce the total interest payments and own your home much sooner.

Twenty Year Mortgage Trend

Mortgage Rate History
From 1970 – 1990 By Year

Percent

Mid Year Rates For Five Year Term

This chart shows a twenty year history of 5 year residential mortgage rates. As you can see, the trend shows an increase from 87 to 90. Presently, mortgage rates may be showing signs of leveling. The future GST will have an effect upon the housing industry. In order to stimulate the housing industry, interest rates will need to decline.

Source: Royal LePage, Residential
   Mortgage Rates

Saving Money On Your Mortgage

19

If you want to save thousands of dollars, you should have an amortization schedule of your mortgage. This schedule shows each monthly payment, beginning with the first payment right through until your mortgage is fully paid. No home owner should be without this schedule.

To see how we can save money on our mortgage, lets look at our previous example of someone holding a $70,000 mortgage at 12%, amortized over 25 years. The monthly payment is $722.33.

In our very first payment of $722.33, we give the mortgage company $683.12 in interest and reduce the balance of our $70,000 loan by $39.21. In month two we make the same monthly payment and reduce our total principle by $39.60 and in month three the non-interest payment is $39.98. Obviously, it will take some time before this mortgage is retired. After we have made 230 payments we are paying $162.48 towards our principle and $359.85 for interest charges.

We would have to make regular payments for just over 19 years before reaching the halfway point of paying off our 25 year mortgage. After this point, more of our money is applied to the principal while fewer dollars go towards interest payments.

The sooner you can begin making extra payments toward your mortgage, even the smallest amount, the faster you can retire the mortgage. Most mortgages allow you to make extra payments on your mortgage and every cent of this payment goes directly towards decreasing the principal.

If you feel it is impossible to make any extra payment towards your mortgage at the end of your first year, be creative in your planning. Set a jar on your dresser and put all the silver from your pocket into the jar every evening.

Bank this silver monthly so you can earn some interest. Remember the parable of the talents; we must be wise with the money entrusted to our care. Pay this money towards your mortgage at year end. You will be pleasantly surprised at how much money you have managed to save by the end of the year.

Another plan may involve establishing a special bank account and having an extra $100.00 transferred into the account each month. At the end of the year, use the money in this savings account to prepay your mortgage.

If you are like my wife and I, you might find you can easily afford to give up one cup of coffee or a donut every day. Not only does my waistline benefit but there is a substantial financial gain waiting for us.

If we turn that $1.25 into a contribution towards our mortgage, we would be able to pay an extra $438.00 towards the mortgage (excluding the interest we would have earned). By paying this money towards our mortgage at the end of month 12, we would have moved down the amortization schedule to about month 19. We would have made 7 months of payments towards the principal and saved $4,738.71 in interest payments. Now that is a good return on your investment.

A very important principle to remember while making extra payments towards your mortgage, is the principle of unity. As the Lord promised: "where two or more come together and agree, I will give them the desires of their heart." As we stressed in our first book,What Every Christian Should Know About Money Management, it is important for families to establish goals together.

There must be unity among husband, wife and children. Where two or more come together and agree, there is very little that can stand in the way of success. I recall one situation where I was visiting a family and the husband said it was his desire to see the mortgage paid off. He said his wife was the problem. She wanted to buy all of Sears' inventory. (His wife probably had a different story.) Obviously there was a problem here because without unity both partners will be going in opposite directions.

It is vital that both husband and wife agree to pay off this mortgage as quickly as possible. By doing so, sacrifices are easier to deal with as the reward becomes more focused with each passing month.

The money you are saving is money you will not have to earn. Also, when you make your monthly payment, you are paying in after tax dollars. The money you are saving is before tax dollars. Therefore, you are making a significant gain because you will not have to pay any taxes on the money that is coming off the pre-payment of your mortgage.

As stewards, we will give an accounting of the property entrusted to our care. Wisdom dictates that we should pay off our mortgage as quickly as possible.

#	DUE DATE	INTEREST	PRINCIPAL	BALANCE OF LOAN
1	FEBRUARY 01, 1991.	683.12	39.21	$ 69,960.79
2	MARCH 01, 1991.	682.73	39.60	$ 69,921.19
3	APRIL 01, 1991.	682.35	39.98	$ 69,881.21
4	MAY 01, 1991.	681.96	40.37	$ 69,840.84
5	JUNE 01, 1991.	681.56	40.77	$ 69,800.07
6	JULY 01, 1991.	681.16	41.17	$ 69,758.90
7	AUGUST 01, 1991.	680.76	41.57	$ 69,717.33
8	SEPTEMBER 01, 1991.	680.36	41.97	$ 69,675.36
9	OCTOBER 01, 1991.	679.95	42.38	$ 69,632.98
10	NOVEMBER 01, 1991.	679.53	42.80	$ 69,590.18
11	DECEMBER 01, 1991.	679.12	43.21	$ 69,546.97
12	JANUARY 01, 1992.	678.69	43.64	$ 69,503.33
13	FEBRUARY 01, 1992.	678.27	44.06	$ 69,459.27
14	MARCH 01, 1992.	677.84	44.49	$ 69,414.78
15	APRIL 01, 1992.	677.40	44.93	$ 69,369.85
16	MAY 01, 1992.	676.97	45.36	$ 69,324.49
17	JUNE 01, 1992.	676.52	45.81	$ 69,278.68
18	JULY 01, 1992.	676.08	46.25	$ 69,232.43
19	AUGUST 01, 1992.	675.63	46.70	$ 69,185.73
20	SEPTEMBER 01, 1992.	675.17	47.16	$ 69,138.57
21	OCTOBER 01, 1992.	674.71	47.62	$ 69,090.95
22	NOVEMBER 01, 1992.	674.24	48.09	$ 69,042.86
23	DECEMBER 01, 1992.	673.78	48.55	$ 68,994.31
24	JANUARY 01, 1993.	673.30	49.03	$ 68,945.28
25	FEBRUARY 01, 1993.	672.82	49.51	$ 68,895.77
26	MARCH 01, 1993.	672.34	49.99	$ 68,845.78
27	APRIL 01, 1993.	671.85	50.48	$ 68,795.30
28	MAY 01, 1993.	671.36	50.97	$ 68,744.33
29	JUNE 01, 1993.	670.86	51.47	$ 68,692.86
30	JULY 01, 1993.	670.36	51.97	$ 68,640.89
31	AUGUST 01, 1993.	669.85	52.48	$ 68,588.41
32	SEPTEMBER 01, 1993.	669.34	52.99	$ 68,535.42
33	OCTOBER 01, 1993.	668.82	53.51	$ 68,481.91
34	NOVEMBER 01, 1993.	668.30	54.03	$ 68,427.88
35	DECEMBER 01, 1993.	667.77	54.56	$ 68,373.32
36	JANUARY 01, 1994.	667.24	55.09	$ 68,318.23

Source: Kissystems, Scarborough, Ontario

Do You Qualify For A Mortgage? **20**

Although many people look forward to buying a house, not everyone can qualify for a mortgage. Financial institutions have fairly tough qualifications each applicant must satisfy to be approved for a house loan.

Requirements may vary slightly among institutions although they all require the following:

1. Letter from employee certifying employment, salary and length of service.

2. Compliance with their interpretation of the Gross Debt Service Ratio. This rather technical term means a lending institution will determine what you can afford to pay for monthly housing costs. This usually includes mortgage payment, interest, taxes and heating. Generally, this amount should not exceed 30 to 32 percent of your gross income.

    If your monthly income is approximately $3,500.00, calculate 30% of your monthly income. This would amount to $1,050.00. That is the amount of money an institution would approve for your combined monthly mortgage, interest, taxes and heating.

3. Another area of concern to some institutions is the size of your total debt, which they refer to as the Total Debt Service Ratio. For this type of debt, your projected housing costs are combined with what you owe

other creditors. The limit to this type of debt is 40 to 42 percent of your gross income.

If your monthly income is $3,500, your total debt load should not exceed $1,400 per month if you wish to qualify for a mortgage.

Frequently, the income of each spouse is taken into consideration. Depending on the institution, heating costs may not be included in the calculations. These ratio's are a quick guide and the final decision is at the discretion of the financial institution.

Shopping For A Pre-Approved Mortgage

21

Shopping for a mortgage is similar to shopping for a car. There are so many models and options to choose from that you often end up buying the first model with a name you can pronounce. Unfortunately, you may end up paying for options you don't quite understand.

One way to avoid "buying" the wrong type of mortgage, is to apply for a pre-approved mortgage at a bank or trust company. This ensures you don't waste time looking at properties you can't afford. The lender will always suggest that you apply for more money than you need. They will argue that you can take less but if you need more you would have to re-apply.

For most of us, this is a dangerous mistake. If you are approved for $10,000 more than you need, you will likely spend it by purchasing a more expensive home or adding a number of options to the house.

If this money is added to the value of your mortgage, you will pay approximately three times the original extra loan in interest or approximately $30,000.00.

Pre-approved mortgages, however, lock you into one company. This can be a disadvantage if another company is offering lower rates, more flexibility or portability for their mortgages. Before you commit to one particular mortgage company, it would be wise to compare what the various mortgage lenders have to offer.

Obviously, mortgage rates will be competitive, but there may be subtle features within the mortgage that are different.

Portable Mortgages

One feature that could save you a lot of money, is a portable mortgage. A portable mortgage moves with you if you buy another home. Without this feature, you would have to cancel your existing mortgage, pay a penalty, and then pay to arrange for a new mortgage. This could be rather expensive, especially if your new mortgage has a higher interest rate than your old mortgage.

If your mortgage will not cover the entire mortgage for the new property, a new mortgage could be blended with the old one and you would still be able to keep your costs lower than if you applied for a whole new mortgage.

Investigate whether you can increase your monthly payments or make lump sum payments against the outstanding principal. Prepaying a mortgage, especially in the early years, can save a substantial amount of money. While most economists argue that we are paying off the mortgage with future dollars which are worth less, it is also satisfying to know you are debt free.

Picking The Right Real Estate Agent **22**

Real estate agents represent the house seller and their task is to get the best price they possibly can for the property. Their commission is paid from the proceeds of the sale so it is in their best interest to obtain the highest price.

If you are buying a house, always bear in mind that the agent's major allegiance is to the seller. Because the agent is representing the seller, any comment you make to the real estate agent will be relayed to the seller. They will let them know how excited you are about the property, what you like or don't like and even how much you might be willing to pay. Bearing this in mind, the best policy is found in Proverbs 16:23 where it says " a wise man's heart guards his mouth."

Even when an agent shows you a house which is listed with a different company, that agent also shares in the commission and is therefore representing the seller.

When you are buying a property, even though the agent is representing the seller, you should still carefully chose the agent which will find you the type of property you want. Consider the following:

1. Attitude. What is the attitude of your agent? Do you feel comfortable trusting this agent with the most money you will likely invest in your lifetime?

2. Full time agents produce results. Many agents work part time and you should make every possible effort to avoid them. You do not want to trust one of the most important financial transactions of your life to someone who is working part time.

3. Deal with an agent who is attentive to your needs and concerns.

4. Is the agent willing to provide references from other people who have purchased a home through him/her?

5. Has the agent negotiated many sales below the advertised selling price? Although an agent's salary is based on commission and therefore the higher the sale the better, if the agent has also made sales below the asking price this indicates that they are flexible and will present your offer with enthusiasm.

House Closing Costs: *23*
The Big Surprise

Now that you have scraped together a down payment, you excitedly await the day to move into that new house. Unless you have planned for "closing costs," your moving day could find you several thousand dollars short and a lawyer who won't give you the keys until you come up with the money.

On the closing date, or date of moving into your new home, you will be faced with a number of costs that vary from province to province. Some provinces charge a deed-transfer tax while others charge a land-transfer tax. Either one can cost you upwards of a thousand dollars.

Some of the other costs you may have to pay your lawyer on closing day include (and there may be more, so ask your lawyer):

1. Fuel costs. If the house is equipped with an oil furnace, the previous owner may have left several hundred dollars worth of fuel in the tank. He expects to be paid for it.

2. Utility costs. Telephone, the hydro, cable and water company, to name a few, will also require either a deposit or hook up fees.

3. Property taxes. The previous owner may have paid the taxes several months ahead. Again, he wants this money back.

4. House repairs. If you have not had an independent house inspector make a careful check of the house, before you agreed to buy it, you may be in for some unpleasant surprises. Perhaps that nice carpeted deck is hiding several hundred dollars worth of rotting boards. They must be replaced before it is safe to use.

   There could be numerous other problems which an independent house inspector could have found before you committed yourself to buying the house. With his report, you could either have continued looking at other houses or used the information as a bargaining measure to lower the asking price of the inspected house. This inspection, by the way, will cost a few hundred dollars but could save you several thousand.

5. Legal fees. This fee could reach $1,000 or more if there are complications.

6. Survey certificate. This will also run into several hundred dollars but is a good idea if the house has not been surveyed for several years.

7. Insurance. The mortgage lender will often insist you provide proof of house insurances before they will issue the mortgage money.

8. Moving expenses. Depending on how far you move and whether your employer is covering the costs or you are moving yourself, this could be quite expensive.

Although closing costs can vary a great deal from province to province or even within a province, they can run as high as 4% of the home's purchase price. Be sure you calculate them far in advance of closing day to ensure your first day in that new home is as pleasant as possible.

Selling Privately Or Using A Broker

24

Selling Private vs. Using a Broker

There is no question that selling a house today can cost you quite a bit of money. If you live in one of Canada's larger metropolitan areas and own a house that is valued at $277,000 (very common for homes in some larger cities), it will cost you $15,240 to sell that house. This is the amount a real estate agent will receive from a 6% commission for selling your property. This is a lot of money so you want to be sure you have a reputable real estate firm and a knowledgeable and successful agent handling the sale.

While 85% of home sales are handled through a real estate company, there is a new and growing trend towards private home sales. To take the guesswork out of selling your home privately, a number of new companies are springing up to offer help to those who wish to go it alone. Since they undercut real estate companies, I suspect they may have a strong future as they launch aggressive advertising campaigns.

Selling your home privately can provide pleasant rewards or contribute to migraine headaches. While the benefit of saving thousands of dollars is attractive, the work involved can be tedious and bothersome. Here are some considerations for you to ponder.

1. Do you have any experience in the area of sales?

2. Do you have experience in marketing, specifically to consumers?

3. Do you know how you will qualify your prospective buyer, to separate the window shoppers from the serious lookers?

4. Consider your understanding and experience of advertising. How much will advertising cost and are you qualified to write up an advertisement?

5. Are you familiar with legal terminology and how to complete an offer to purchase?

6. Be prepared for no-shows and a flow of real estate agents calling for your listing and telling you they have a prospective buyer for your home. When you decline their offer for a listing, experience has taught me they can be rude, ignorant, childish and totally unprofessional.

7. Do you have the time required to work at selling your house on a full-time basis?

Should you decide that selling your house is more bother than it is worth, your only alternative is a real estate company. If you decide to use a broker, be careful to pick a real estate agent with whom you feel comfortable. Here are some additional considerations for you to ponder as well.

Selecting A Real Estate Company

1. Find a company with a proven track record of success. You can acquire names from friends and neighbours as well as take notice of the companies with the largest numbers of sold signs throughout your community. At the same time, remember that the sold sign usually show the company that originated the listing and not necessarily the company who actually sold the property.

2. Have the company provide you with a marketing plan for selling your house. This includes advertising and promotion, agent viewing and open houses.

3. What is the company's attitude? Are the agents self motivated and successful at making sales? Remember a winner does not make excuses.

4. Does the company regularly advertise in the local and out-of-town papers?

5. Will the company provide references, including telephone numbers, from previous clients?

6. Is the company a local business, well known and respected in your community?

7. Has the company grown in size during the past two years or have they become smaller?

Real estate companies sign an agreement to sell a property. The listing agreement is binding on both the seller and the company. This agreement in effect, binds all the agents of that company to represent the seller.

Selecting An Agent

To ensure that you are assigned an agent who has your best interests at heart, there are a number of points you should consider before agreeing to take a particular agent. These would include:

1. Experience.

2. Successful track record.

3. Usually sells properties within 5% of the listing price.

4. Proven leader in their company.

5. Reputation for excellence and follow through.

6. References from previous clients.

7. Avoid the listing agent. While they list a number of homes to sell, they often wait for someone else to sell the property. Regardless of who sells the house, the listing agent receives a commission. This type of agent seldom gives good service.

If you are not satisfied with your agent, ask the company for another representative.

Make Your Mortgage Tax Deductible

25

You have been living in your home now for several years. That small pine tree you planted when you first moved in, is now the same size as your 10-year-old daughter. Your mortgage will be paid off in 12 more years and you have made some good investments for the "golden" years.

Like other Canadians, you make monthly, bi-weekly or weekly mortgage payments. Payments are made from your after tax employment income or what economists call "after tax dollars."

You should now consider selling your investments and paying down the mortgage. Depending on how much money you have invested, you might even be able to pay off the entire mortgage.

Once you have reduced your mortgage, or paid it off, use the equity in your home as security and borrow funds to buy back your investments. The interest you will pay on these borrowed funds is tax deductible, because they have been used for investment purposes. This is in contrast to the interest you paid on your mortgage which was not tax deductible.

You come out a winner. You save money on your mortgage by not having to pay thousands of dollars in interest. You can also earn investment income and the interest costs can be deducted from this income.

Whether you pay off the entire mortgage or a portion of your mortgage, you come out ahead. At the end of year one assume you have $5,000 to invest, and you are not sure whether to invest in a term deposit or put your money into your mortgage.

$5,000 in a term deposit produces the following:

Amount Invested	$5,000.
Interest Earned @ 10%	$ 500.
Taxes On Interest@ 40%	$ 200.
Net Income	$ 300.

The same $5,000 applied against your $50,000 mortgage which is costing you 11.75% calculated semi-annually would produce the following, if invested at the end of your first year. Not only do you save money, but, you reduce the number of years required to pay off the mortgage by almost eight (8) years.

Amount Invested	$ 5,000.
Total Saved	$48,186.
Taxes On Money Saved	Nil
Net Savings	$48,186.

Source: Your Money and how to keep it.
    Brian Costello, Stoddart, Toronto, 1990.

Counting On An Accountant

26

The Canadian tax structure operates on the honour system. We complete our tax return with the understanding that we are telling the truth.

Sometimes we make honest mistakes. Revenue Canada is quite understanding about these type of errors. The other kind, dishonest ones, could cost you a lot of money.

The problem facing most Canadians is that they do not understand the tax forms. Recent changes to the forms contribute to this dilemma. Consequently, people are unsure of what they should report and what does not need reporting. As a result, you could be paying too much income tax.

For the Christian, there is no option at Income Tax time. We have a moral obligation to report accurately when filing our return. We read in Romans, "Everyone must submit himself to the governing authorities, for there is no authority except that which God has established. The authorities that exist have been established by God."

To avoid over-payments and errors, accountants can be very helpful. I am not an accountant, but I encourage anyone who suspects that their tax return is not a regular run-of-the-mill return, to see an accountant.

Accountants provide a variety of services. They will assess business ventures, prepare proposals for banks, give a critique of your business. They also prepare and interpret financial statements. Accountants prepare both corporate and personal tax returns. They are also an additional source of investment advice. "Plans fail for a lack of counsel, but with many advisers they succeed."(Pr.15:22)

If you operate your own business, you likely need an accountant. Whether your business is part-time or full-time, big or small, wisdom suggests visiting an accountant. Accountants charge their clients according to the amount of work involved. Experience has shown me that they are affordable and can save you a pile of money and grief.

If you do not have an accountant, ask your friends if they could recommend someone, or ask at your church. Tax accountants prepare hundreds of tax returns each year. We normally prepare one and sometimes two. Definitely a case for accountants and the phrase,"practice makes perfect."

An important verse to remember is found in Mark 12. Give to Caesar what is his and to God what is His.

Income Splitting: There is Still Hope

27

It is often said that two people can live cheaper than one. While experience usually proves otherwise, a process called "income splitting" means two finally can live cheaper than one.

When possible, it is usually wise to split incomes between the higher wage earner and lower wage earner within a family. In some cases, the lower wage earner might be a spouse who works at home raising and caring for the children.

We have a two tier tax system in Canada. First, you calculate your Federal Tax and then add a Provincial Tax based on a percentage of the Federal Tax.

You combine the Federal and the Provincial tax rates to determine your marginal rate of tax. The provincial rates vary, but the following will serve to give a rough indication of your marginal rate of tax.

1989 Approximate Tax Rate

Tax is 27% of income up to $27,800

Tax is 41% of income up to $55,600

Tax is 45% on income in excess of $55,600

For example, tax payable on an income of $38,059 would be calculated as follows:

27% of the first 27,800 = $7,506

41% of the remaining $10,259 = $4,206

Total due   = $7,506 + $4,206 = $11,712

If we were able to split the income between two spouses in even portions, the following would result.

Income $38,059/2 = $19,030 each

Tax on 19,030 at 27% = $5,138

Both spouses would end up paying the same amount of tax because their income would now be equal. The total taxes due would then amount to $5,138 x 2 = $10,276 not taking into account surtaxes charged.

Savings = $11,712 - $10,276 = $1,436

While income splitting saved some couples a lot of money in the past, Revenue Canada took steps in previous budgets to tighten up on this form of tax savings. Here are some options, however, which are still available to help spouses split their income.

1. Invest the monthly family allowance check in your children's names. Have them report the income they earn since it is unlikely they will pay any tax. Consequently, a parent will not have to pay tax on the income earned.

2. Have the spouse with the higher income pay expenses incurred by the lower income earner and all household expenses. This leaves more money for investment in the hands of the lower income earner who will be taxed at a lower rate on investment income.

3. Utilize spousal RRSP's. The income earner with the higher income will receive current tax relief, by buying an RRSP for the lower wage earner. When the money is withdrawn from the plan, the lower wage earner will be taxed at a lower rate.

4. If you own a small business and can arrange to hire your spouse to manage or operate the business, you can easily split your incomes.

5. If you own a small business, you can also employ your children. While they will pay tax on their income, it will be at a lower rate. By paying their children, a parent will not have to take money out of their own pocket to buy the children's clothes etc. Because the children are earning their own money they can buy what they need while the parent will be taxed at a lower rate.

Federal/Provincial Income Tax

28

We have a two tier tax system in Canada. First, you calculate your Federal Tax. Then you add a Provincial Tax which is based on a percentage of the Federal Tax.

You combine the Federal and the Provincial tax rates to determine your marginal rate of tax. This is the amount of tax you pay on your last dollar earned. It sounds more complicated than it actually is.

The following rates are based on the 1989 Federal and Provincial Income Tax Rates:

Federal Rates	Range Of Income	Amount Of Tax Payable
17%	$0 - $27,803	$0 - $4,726
26%	$27,803 - $55,605	$4,726 + 26% on amount over $27,803
29%	$55,605 and over	$4,726 + $7,229 + 29% on amount over $55,605

In the chart below, note that besides the three Federal rates of 17%, 26% and 29%, you get to pay the province a percentage as well. The provincial rate is based on the amount of federal tax payable. So, if your federal tax is $10,000, the province wants their percentage - thank you very much - based on the $10,000.

Province	Provincial Rate	17%+	26%+	29%+
Alberta	46.5%	24.91%	38.0%	42.5%
British Columbia	51.5%	25.76%	39.39%	43.94%
Manitoba	52.0%	25.84%	39.52%	44.08%
New Brunswick	60.0%	27.20%	41.60%	46.40%
NewFoundland	61.0%	27.37%	41.86%	46.69%
Northwest Territories	43.0%	24.31%	37.18%	41.47%
Nova Scotia	56.5%	26.61%	40.69%	45.39%
Ontario	52.0%	25.84%	39.52%	44.08%
Prince Edward Island	57.0%	26.69%	40.82%	45.53%
Quebec	Not A Flat Rate			
Saskatchewan	50.0%	25.5%	39.00%	43.50%
Yukon	45.0%	24.65%	37.70%	42.05%

By selecting your province or territory and your approximate income level, you can get a quick snapshot of your possible tax liability. Under the Federal rates of 17%, 26% and 29% (calculated above), we have included the provincial rates to arrive at the total tax bite. The above does not take into account any Federal or Provincial surtaxes which will take another chunk out of your pocket.

Non-Taxable Income

29

Although we are to give unto Caesar what is Caesar's, don't include money which is not his when filling out your income tax forms. The following is a list of some of the items that are tax free.

- child tax credits
- federal sales tax credits
- lottery winnings
- veteran's disability and dependents' pension payments
- life insurance revenue
- war veteran's allowances
- inheritances
- first $100,000 capital gains (must be reported then deducted)
- money received from the sale of your home (principal residence)
- workers' compensation benefits
- welfare and social assistance programs
- net federal supplements paid (includes spouse's allow ance and guaranteed income supplement)
- income from children's aid

It Sometimes Pays To Move

30

Canadians are about the most move happy people in the world. It seems they no sooner put down roots than they pull them up again for a move to greener pastures. If you do it right though, your next move could be worth money.

If you decide to move to a different part of Canada to begin a new job, start a business or continue working for your present employer, the government will help you on the way.

Given certain restrictions, you may deduct your moving expenses if the move meets two criteria. First, it must relate to a job change. Secondly, the move must be more than 40 km's from your present address. Assuming you qualify you will enjoy significant deductions.

You may claim any or possibly all the following expenses.

Real Estate Fees	Legal Fees
Storage Costs	Moving Expenses
Packing Expenses and/or storage	Insurance for moving
Land Transfer Taxes	Temporary Accomodation
Airline Tickets	Gasoline
Food	Terminating A Lease
Telephone Connection	Cable TV Connection

Keep careful records of your out-of-pocket expenses as well as any of the above noted items. You will be required to produce receipts to support your claims. The expenses are deducted from your income earned at the new location of employment.

Students qualify for moving expenses if they travel more than 40Km's to a post-secondary institution.

You should also bear in mind that, depending on where you move, your taxes could go up or down. We pay provincial taxes based on where we live as of December 31. If you live in a province with a high tax rate and move during December to a province with a lower rate, you win.

If you move from a province with a lower rate to a higher rate province, you lose. Best to delay your move in this case until January 1.

Family Allowance: A Family Affair

31

The family allowance payment is a welcome sight each month. While many families use the money to buy the children's clothing, it would be a good idea to consider investing this money. Let's consider both options:

Buying the Children's Clothing

1. When filling out their income tax return, many parents report family allowance cheques as part of their personal income.

2. The family allowance cheques could put you into a higher tax bracket. The fact that you used the money to purchase the children's clothing is irrelevant to the government. They will still tax you on this money.

Investing the Money

1. If you place the money in a bank account or other type of investment, in your child's name, the child claims the money as income, rather than the parent.

2. Children are allowed to earn $2,528.00 (as of 1989) tax-free per year. Your child is probably not earning more than $2,528.00 so they will not have to pay income tax on this money.

Watching the Money Grow

1. Assume that the average family allowance payment is $35.00 per month or $420.00 yearly.

2. If this money earned an average of 10%, compounded yearly, it would accumulate in excess of $21,000 in 18 years. The money received through family allowance payments is $7,560.00. This money may earn $13,635.00 in tax free interest when held in the name of your child.

Teaching Children About Money

32

As I travel across Canada, one of the most common statements I hear following our seminars is, "I wish I knew this years ago." Hindsight is always perfect vision.

The Bible says, "Train a child in the way he should go and when he is old he will not turn from it." (Pr. 22:6)

Most people want to determine their own choices in life, but frequently they are prevented from doing so by a lack of funds. A lack of funds is usually the result of poor training or no training at all.

While Christian parents have the responsibility to raise their children to respect and honour God in all areas of life, we often neglect the area of finances. As Christians, we should be at the forefront of teaching our children about the importance and role of money, the discipline of regular giving and the habit of saving money. These characteristics are not inherent, they are learned and therefore need to be taught.

If we do not teach our children about money, who will teach them? Can we rely on the educational system to do the job? As a former teacher, I can assure you teachers have their hands full teaching the basics. We should not expect someone else to shoulder the responsibility of teaching our children the subjects we choose to neglect.

Why don't we spend time teaching our children about money and money management? There are a number of reasons but I suspect the following might be some of the reasons:

- we feel inadequate
- we have not been financially successful
- we don't know where to start
- we have not given it that much consideration
- we have not taken the time to educate ourselves about money and financial management

Where should we start, if we want to remedy the situation? When do we start? The Bible has much to say about money and money management.

Start by reading passages from the Bible and determine what God would have you do with your money. A good place to start is researching God's attitude toward tithing.

Set an example for your children, teaching them to research the Bible for answers to everyday financial situations.

Set a positive example by becoming a role model for your children to see and respect.

Involve children in some of the financial discussions and decisions affecting your family.

Establish an allowance for your children and encourage them to tithe and share from their allowance.

Allow your children to spend their money on items they want. Encourage them to evaluate a purchase and save their money until they are able to afford the item.

If a particular transaction or purchase goes sour, do not scold or chastise the child, Use the situation to teach alternative decisions they could consider. At the same time, give your child positive reinforcement when they make a good decision.

Approach this subject with an attitude of fun. You are free to be creative. Consider rewarding your children for special tasks they perform over and above what is required to generate their allowance. Look for stimulating incentives. Although this idea did not originate with me, I once paid my children for every book of the Bible they read and summarized on paper.

What a blessing, my children received extra income for their enjoyment and learned principles that will sustain them for a lifetime.

Finding A Good Insurance Agent

33

Ask most people what word first comes to mind when they think of insurance and they often choose the word, confusing. Whether the insurance is life, property, disability, auto, accident, liability, bill payment insurance or dozens of other types, many people feel they don't understand the subject and therefore often forget about it.

Experience has shown me that many people are under insured, have policies they can't understand and don't know who to call for help. Why is this the case? Perhaps it is the high turnover in sales representatives so that we seldom deal with the same agent on a long term basis. Many people also find insurance policies intimidating because of the language and legal terms used throughout most policies.

Another reason for bewilderment is the fact that we buy insurance and within two or three years we can't remember the terms and conditions of what we purchased.

Now is a good time to consider some of the basic questions you need to consider when reviewing your insurance needs.

The Insurance Agent: Friend or Enemy

There is no substitute for a qualified, reliable and trustworthy insurance agent. Like all professions, there are good agents and there are agents who may place their own needs ahead of your best interest. This can lead to people buying the wrong type of policy, buying too much or not enough coverage or not receiving adequate service or follow-up from the sales agent.

When you decide to purchase insurance, it's important to remember that there is a difference between an insurance agent and an insurance broker. An agent is limited to the products his company offers. The broker can sell products from a variety of companies, provided he has made a prior arrangement with them.

The broker offers several advantages by allowing comparison shopping among a number of companies. A broker can then tailor a policy with the price, flexibility and service required to meet your needs.

If you find your agent is not knowledgeable and unable to advise you properly, it might be a good time to shop around for a new agent. You may find that you are better off with a good agent from a small company than to remain with a good company staffed by bad agents. When looking for a reliable insurance agent, consider the following:

1. Experience! Does your agent have enough insurance experience to handle your current and future needs? If you or your wife require a simple term policy, then perhaps any agent can meet your needs. However, if you want estate planning, retirement planning, or wish to purchase annuities or establish a group policy for your company, then you will need an experienced agent.

2. Knowledge! Is your agent currently taking courses, attending seminars or reading-up on the latest changes in taxation, insurance products or retirement planning? A knowledgeable agent is well versed and well read on coming trends and current attitudes which may affect their clients.

3. Integrity! There is no substitute for honesty and integrity. Can you trust your agent to carry out your wishes after you die? Will the agent assist your spouse in their critical time of need?

4. Reliability! A successful agent is one who is reliable. Does the agent have a track record of doing what they promise? Successful agents do not use or need excuses.

5. Contemporary thinker! It is imperative for the successful agent to be up-to-date in their office automation. Having access to computers, the most current estate planning software, fax machines and remote telephones, can save their clients time and trouble.

6. Service! In our fast-paced world, service seems to be a quality many of us remember but few of us seldom experience. With the trend in the retail industry to "self service," too many companies feel servicing is an old fashioned concept. It is rare to find someone who will provide service that includes regular follow-up, a review of our needs or advice on product changes. Fewer still publish a regular newsletter to ensure their clients receive this information on a regular basis.

If you find an insurance agent who fills the above bill, you should hang onto him.

Insurance: How Much Do You Need?

34

The purpose of insurance is to protect your family from financial loss when a wage earner dies or is disabled.

The severity of losing a paycheck becomes obvious when the mortgage or rent must be paid, groceries bought or regular household expenses have to be met.

The amount of required insurance will vary, depending on each family's need. Following is a brief summary to estimate your particular needs. Each income earner in the family should complete this form and review it on a regular basis.

Example	Your Income	
Annual Income Before Taxes	$_____	$50,000
Amount Family Needs (Allow approximately 75% of income as their needs after your death)	$_____	$37,500
Deduct Annual Canada Pension Plan Benefits.(This is replaced by CPP Survivors Pension)	$_____	-$6,000*
Amount Of Income Required Annually	$_____	$31,500
Insurance Needed To Generate Annual Income. (Assume 10% interest earned on investments)	$_____	$315,000

* The amount of CCP benefits will vary according to your particular situation.

The total amount of your insurance needs may include a group policy at work. Remember, if your job situation changes you may have to increase your personal insurance policy.

Source: Woodhouse Executive Insurance,
        Newmarket

Your Will Has Power

35

Many people feel they don't need a Will. If you are among this group, consider the following questions. Your answers might change your mind. Answer them quickly and honestly.

1. Have you protected your family by making out a Will?

2. Does your family know where you keep your important papers?

3. If you died tonight, would there be enough money available to provide for your family's immediate and long term needs?

4. If you have prepared a Will, does it reflect your current thinking?

5. Does your executor know your wishes pertaining to your funeral?

If you answered no to any of these questions, you have some work to do. Most Canadians have not prepared their Will and therefore have no arrangements for the orderly disposal of their assets.

Someday, someone else will own everything you have worked years to acquire. You have a responsibility to disperse of these assets in an effective way which also honours God.

Here are some suggestions to consider when drawing up your Will.

1. Use a lawyer. Avoid the do-it-yourself Will. Lawyers are trained professionals who can provide a document to suit your particular needs.

2. Before drafting your Will, ask someone to be your executor. If you are married, your spouse will likely be your executor or executrix. Consider an alternate choice, so if something happens to prevent your first choice from carrying out your wishes, you do not need to rewrite the entire Will. Your alternate choice will carry out the duties of your executor.

3. If you have minor children, consider who you and your spouse would like to care for them. Obviously you will select someone who shares your values and beliefs. Unless you select someone, the provincial government will make the decision.

4. In Proverbs 3:9,10, we read that we are to honour the Lord with our wealth and our firstfruits. After we have fulfilled this requirement, the verse goes on to say "your barns will be filled to overflowing, and your vats will brim over with new wine." It is clear that when we take the first step, God will do His part.

I encourage you to consider leaving a gift to charitable work in your Will. It has been estimated that of the thirty percent of the population who have completed a will, less than five percent have made provisions for a gift to support Christian work. This means that only about one and a half percent of the population leave anything to Christian charity.

A deferred gift in our Christian Will makes both economic sense and is in keeping with Scripture. After all, Jesus Himself is the perfect example of a deferred gift. He died two thousand years ago for our benefit today.

5. Although a Will is the starting point, for some people it is not enough. They may need to establish a testa-

mentary trust. A trust, established through you Will, could provide for the special care of someone who is handicapped, a minor, grandchildren or provide for charity work or any other reason you may consider.

Do You Need A Will?

The short answer to this question is that everyone should have a Will. Some, however, may feel they don't have enough money or assets to bother with a Will.

Taking care of the assets entrusted to our care is important. How much you have is not as important as what do you do with what you do have. Christians are reminded of the story of the widow's mite. Jesus noted that although she gave only three cents, she gave more than everyone else because it was everything she had.

If any of the following situations apply to you, then you need to consider preparing your Will.

- You do not presently have a Will.

- You were recently married/divorced.

- You are a widow/widower.

- You have not reviewed your Will for three to five years.

- You wish to leave some money to your favourite charities/special friends.

- You have received a large sum of money.

- You recently became a parent.

- You have someone in the family who will need special care in the future.

- Your Will does not reflect your current thinking.

It is wise to use a lawyer in preparing your Will. It is best to avoid do-it-yourself wills from stationery stores or attempt to write your own. Lawyers are well versed in writing Wills and they can help you accomplish your individual goals.

Earning Money After You Are Gone

36

While Christians are spiritually prepared for death, they are seldom prepared financially. Although you can not take your money with you, and who would want to, you can ensure that what you leave behind continues to benefit others.

Consider the following questions to determine if you are prepared financially for death. If you unexpectedly died now, would your family:

1. Have enough money to continue in their present lifestyle?

2. Understand financial matters sufficiently to handle your estate?

3. Know where to find your Will?

Most Christians have not prepared any estate plans and for the most part, are not prepared for a sudden or expected death. Death occurs at all ages and is not reserved for the old. At the same time, just because you are prepared for death from a financial perspective, doesn't mean you are going to die any sooner. It just means that your death will not cause any more grief than is necessary.

In Canada, approximately six out of ten Christians have not bothered to prepare a simple Will. A Will provides many benefits. You spend a lifetime gathering and accumulating assets, you should have some say in how they will be dispersed.

If you do not prepare a Will, the rules for dispersement are outlined by the province where you lived and you may be disappointed by the way they dispose of your assets.

Frequently, we hear mention of a Christian Will. The difference between a Christian and non-Christian Will is that the Christian Will honours the Lord with a gift to carry on His work. This enables the Church and various ministries to carry out their mandate.

In order to determine our wealth, we prepare a balance sheet. This is a record of what we owe and what we own. The difference between the two is our equity or net worth. Our wealth is that amount which we have accumulated over the years and are now using as we wish.

Our wealth is the accumulation of our investments, our houses, our summer homes, our recreational equipment, savings and many other possessions. When we prepare a Will that honours the Lord with a gift from our wealth, we are acknowledging His rightful ownership and our stewardship of His wealth.

If we are to honour the Lord from this wealth, then one important step is to make a deferred gift in our Will to help carry on Christian work. A deferred gift honours God while not depriving us of any money. After all, we will leave it all behind at death.

A Will not only gives us peace of mind, it also allows us to continue participating in the work we supported during our life. If we die intestate (without a Will), the various organizations which we supported, as well as our friends and relatives, might not receive a gift. If they were to receive a gift, it may not be what we would consider the proper proportion so that others might receive more than those who have the greater need.

While Scriptures do not specifically state "leave a deferred gift to my work", Jesus is the perfect example of a deferred gift. He died two thousand years ago for our benefit today. When we are told to honour the Lord from our wealth and when we consider the example Jesus set for us, I feel the Christian community should be excited about the opportunity to make a deferred gift to His work.

When you decide to use your Will to honour God(Pr.3:9) you involve yourself, your Will and God.

For the purpose of illustration we will refer to the three major types as the Common Will, Common Will With Gift To Charity and The Innovative Will. For the sake of simplicity, in the Innovative Will we have not illustrated any taxes owed by the Trust. These taxes would need to be paid and this could cause the doubling effect to take just a little longer than illustrated. The important consideration is the concept as it can be altered to accommodate any situation.

1. The Common Will

This Will is the type many choose. It is simple, straight forward and leaves all assets to the surviving partner in a family. When the parents die, all assets left are divided equally among the children. Nothing is left to Christian ministry. An estate of $350,000 would pay out this amount of money, minus administration fees.

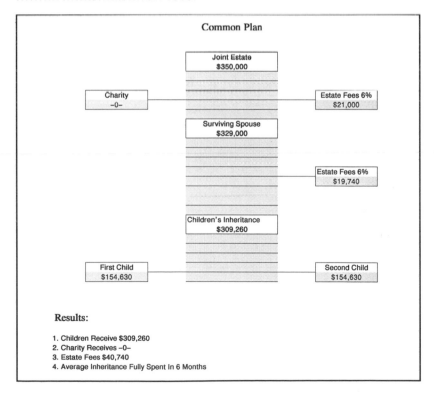

Common Plan

Joint Estate $350,000

Charity –0–

Estate Fees 6% $21,000

Surviving Spouse $329,000

Estate Fees 6% $19,740

Children's Inheritance $309,260

First Child $154,630

Second Child $154,630

Results:

1. Children Receive $309,260
2. Charity Receives –0–
3. Estate Fees $40,740
4. Average Inheritance Fully Spent In 6 Months

2. The Common Will With Gift To Charity

This Will is the same as The Common Will, except a gift has been earmarked for Christian ministry or a charity. Again, a $350,000 estate would pay out $350,000 minus administration fees.

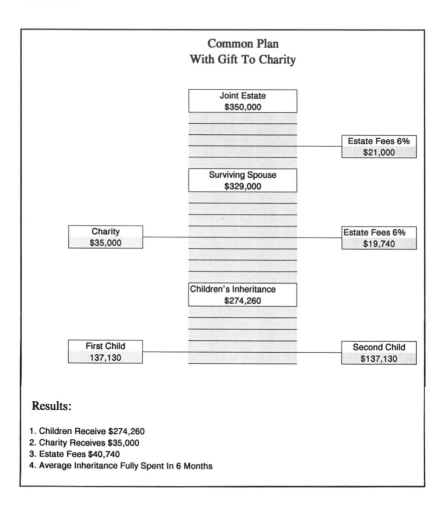

**Common Plan
With Gift To Charity**

Joint Estate $350,000	
	Estate Fees 6% $21,000
Surviving Spouse $329,000	
Charity $35,000	Estate Fees 6% $19,740
Children's Inheritance $274,260	
First Child 137,130	Second Child $137,130

Results:

1. Children Receive $274,260
2. Charity Receives $35,000
3. Estate Fees $40,740
4. Average Inheritance Fully Spent In 6 Months

3. The Innovative Will

This is the type of Will which most people would insist upon if they were aware of how their money could be multiplied. Under this plan, a $350,000 estate could pay out a total of $585,000. Although there are several ways to establish this type of Will, one common plan would be to establish a trust fund which would pay out a set amount each year. Over the course of this fund, an amount almost equal to the estate would be paid out while the principal amount would be left intact. The following figures graphically illustrates the superiority of this type of Will.

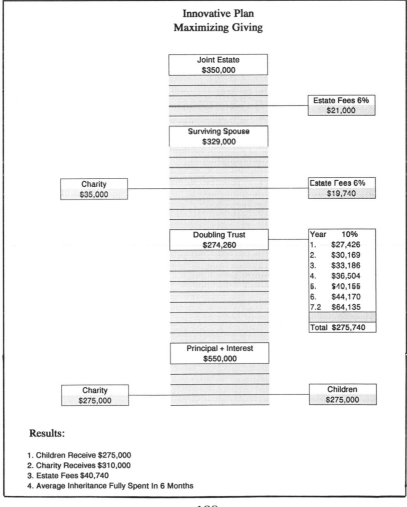

Innovative Plan
Maximizing Giving

Joint Estate
$350,000

Estate Fees 6%
$21,000

Surviving Spouse
$329,000

Charity
$35,000

Estate Fees 6%
$19,740

Doubling Trust
$274,260

Year	10%
1.	$27,426
2.	$30,169
3.	$33,186
4.	$36,504
5.	$40,155
6.	$44,170
7.2	$64,135
Total	$275,740

Principal + Interest
$550,000

Charity
$275,000

Children
$275,000

Results:

1. Children Receive $275,000
2. Charity Receives $310,000
3. Estate Fees $40,740
4. Average Inheritance Fully Spent In 6 Months

Planning Retirement

37

The Why And Wherefore of Retirement Planning

If you wait until you are 60 to plan for your retirement, you have probably waited too long. Many individuals will reach retirement age and realize they should have spent more time planning because their finances are totally inadequate. As the saying goes, "once the horse has left the barn it is pretty difficult to lock him in."

It is likely that you will live to enjoy your retirement years, most people do. If you continue to save for your retirement at the same rate you have saved during the past five years, how much money will you have at retirement? Will it allow you to maintain your present lifestyle or will you be forced to make a substantial cut?

Why Plan for retirement?

1. You will likely reach retirement age

2. We usually face a decrease in income during retirement

3. It will help us adjust to a new lifestyle

4. Planning helps us stay young and active

How To Plan For Retirement?

1. Evaluate your present lifestyle

2. Evaluate present sources of income that will carry into the future

3. Evaluate future supplementary sources of income

4. Determine a possible date for retirement

5. Prepare a retirement budget based on projected needs

6. Adjust your budget and income to allow for inflation

7. Secure low risk investments

8. Decide how much money you will you need upon retirement

Sources Of Income At Retirement

1. Private Pension Plans

2. Company Provided Pension Plans

3. Canada Pension Plan

4. Supplemental Pensions, Old Age Security Pension

5. Personal Investments

6. Annuities or Registered Retirement Income Funds

7. Family Home

Guidelines On Planning For Retirement

Although many of us look forward to retirement, few of us actively plan for retirement day. Planning for our retirement is important, however, if we want to enjoy security and freedom in the retirement years. Quality planning now means our retirement will allow us to enjoy freedom from time commitments while accomplishing new personal goals.

One major consideration in retirement planning, is to calculate the amount of money you will need after receiving that last regular pay check. Frequently, we become complacent and decide to wait until we are older before considering how much money we will need during our retirement years. This is a mistake. The sooner you plan and work towards accomplishing your retirement plan, the more chance you actually have of attaining financial security for your retirement years.

Following are some guidelines to start you on the road to planning for the retirement years:

1. Estimate how much money you will need when you retire. Don't forget to include a factor to allow for inflation. As a general rule, try to plan for at least seventy percent of your present income.

In order to accomplish this, you will require a concise budget. In my book, What Every Christian Should Know About Money Management, I detailed how to establish a budget while taking inflation into account. You could use the forms at the back of this book or design your own forms.

A budget is a basic necessity in preparing any financial plan. Since it is considered basic, most people tend to skip over this part. One of the major purposes of your budget is to itemize present expenses to determine whether they will decrease or increase in the future.

Equal importance should be given to regularly reviewing your budget and making any changes which arise.

2. Examine all your sources of income during retirement. There are five major sources to consider.

    - Employer Pension Plans
    - Government Pension Plans
    - Personal Investments
    - Personal Pension Plans and Retirement Savings
    - Family Home

Now we will examine each of these in more detail:

(A)   Employer Pension Plans are part of the benefit package most companies offer and vary from company to company. The most common plan is a defined pension plan which is based on your age and years of service. There is normally a penalty if you decide to retire early. This penalty could vary from 1 to 2 percent of your entire benefit, for each year you retire before the normal retirement age.

If you do decide to take early retirement, be sure to include the reduced amount of income into your budget projections.

(B)   Government Pension provisions will not likely be sufficient on their own. With an aging population and a decreasing work force, this plan is facing reduced pension revenues and possibly a decrease in benefits.

(C)   Personal investments can be a good source of income, provided you have the money to invest. As you approach retirement, investment portfolios can provide potential for capital gains and a good measure of security. The closer you are to retirement the less likely you are to engage in high risk investment.

(D)   Personal registered retirement savings plans will help make up any shortfall in income from both your employer and the government. The money invested in your RRSP will not be taxed until you withdraw the money. If you withdraw the funds after your retirement when your income has decreased, you may pay tax at a lower rate.

The sooner you purchase an RRSP, the better. Consider establishing a spousal RRSP. When you contribute to your spouse's plan, you will receive a tax deduction. Money is placed into their account and you are setting the stage for future income splitting. The more income you can split with your spouse the better your cash flow and the lower your tax obligation.

(E)   For some people, their home will provide them with retirement funds. Since a house is our primary residence, we are not charged any tax when we sell this asset. As we

113

grow older, the maintenance and general upkeep on a home can become strenuous. We must rely on others to carry out certain functions and usually at their convenience.

Selling the family home and finding smaller accommodations is something to seriously consider. Even after this move, you would have some money left over to apply towards your retirement.

However, we do not necessarily receive all the money from the sale of our house to put towards our retirement income. For example, if we sold a house for $180,000.00, we will need some of that money to pay for other accommodations. If we paid $120,000.00 for a condominium or smaller home, we are left with $60,000.00.

If the $60,000.00 dollars is invested at ten percent, we would receive $6,000.00 before tax dollars every year. If we paid a combined federal and provincial tax rate of 25.5%, or $1,530.00 in tax, this would leave us with $4,470.00 or $372.50 a month.

Knowing your financial needs upon retirement and the sources and approximate amounts of income available to you, can help you determine when you should retire.

Here are some of the factors which may affect your decision to retire.

- Your age and normal life expectancy
- Your present state of health
- Employer pension regulations
- Desire for lifestyle changes
- Amount of funds available for retirement use

Pension Facts At A Glance

	1990	
	Canada Pension Plan	Quebec Pension Plan
Yearly Maximum Pensionable Earnings	$28,900	$28,900
Yearly Basic Exemption	$ 2,800	$ 2,800
Maximum Annual Contributions		
Employee	$574.20	$574.20
Employer	$574.20	$574.20
Retirement Benefits		
Maximum Monthly Pension	$577.08	$577.08
Survivor (Death) Benefits		
Lump Sum	$ 2,890	$ 2,890
Spousal Pension		
under age 55	$324.37	$493.12
age 55-65	$324.37	$570.42
over 65	$346.25	$346.25
Orphan's Pension		
Each Child/Monthly	$107.96	$ 29.00
Disability Benefits		
Contributor's Pension/Monthly	$709.52	$709.52
Child's Pension/Monthly	$107.96	$ 29.00

The Golden Years Can Be Busy Years

38

I remember a lady who lived in the house behind us. I would see her out every day walking to the grocery store or just walking for exercise. It didn't matter if it was raining or snowing she would be out every day walking at an extremely fast pace.

One day I stopped her and asked why she always walked so fast? After all, she was in her nineties. Her answer surprised me. She said she walked as fast as she could in order to keep her balance. She was afraid that if she slowed down she would fall over.

I was not sure if this was the best reason for walking fast, but, she lived to be over one hundred. You can't argue with success.

There is no substitute for good health. It would appear that one of the factors leading to proper health in our senior years is activity. Not only will activity keep us involved but it will help us maintain a young attitude.

Fitness is a blend of physical, social and spiritual activities.

Physical Activities

Your program could include any regular exercise outside the home such as walking, playing golf, jogging or other activities which you enjoy. Don't get caught up in any type of activity which becomes boring or holds little interest for you.

When we examine the lives of leaders in the Old Testament,

we see numerous examples of people engaged in physical activities. Imagine having Caleb as one of your generals, still in active military service at 80 years of age.

In the New Testament, the best example is Jesus. During His ministry, Jesus travelled from city to city by walking. Not only was there a heavy demand on His time and energy but the large crowds following Him probably make it awkward to move about.

Physical fitness is frequently determined by our attitude. We must maintain a positive attitude about the things we do and the physical activity that occupies our time. It is easier to sit around and do nothing. Healthy and active people would rather move around and seek creative ways to keep them busy.

Be sure to consult a doctor before engaging in any type of exercise program and maintain regular physical check-ups.

Social Activities

The Bible is very strong on the point of enjoying fellowship with other believers. Social interaction helps keep us alert and involved with our surroundings.

Social activity helps to promote a youthful attitude. I once asked my mother if she would like to go out to a restaurant for lunch. I remember her reply. She said, "don't ask, the answer today, tomorrow and forever is yes." Now I call to advise my mother when we are going for lunch knowing I have a date.

The church provides many social functions for seniors. If your church does not offer functions you would like to attend, perhaps there are other people who feel as you do. Offer to implement a new social gathering, travel program or a series of tours for seniors.

Develop hobbies now. These activities will provide years of enjoyment in the future. It is important to develop activities you enjoy and share these things with others.

Spiritual Fitness

Spiritual fitness is vital to enjoying life. We clearly need to continue growing in our Christian understanding. The seniors of this country have a wealth of knowledge and wisdom that needs to be shared with the younger generation.

It is important to attend Bible study classes and to participate in various programs and functions throughout the church.

Benefits For Seniors

39

This section appeared in my first book, "What Every Christian Should Know About Money Management." The response to the book and this particular section indicated the need and importance of this information. For that reason, I felt it would be beneficial to repeat and update the information for this book.

SERVICES AVAILABLE TO SENIORS

National

In Canada there are three pension and retirement income programs available to seniors. There is the Canada Pension Plan, Old Age Security and Guaranteed Income Supplement. These are listed below with a brief description and directions for obtaining information and assistance.

1. Canada Pension Plan

This plan provides for you and your family against loss of earnings when you retire (as well as if you become disabled or die). The plan is based on annual contributions paid by you and your employer.

The plan provides for a regular monthly payment upon retirement. Payments can begin at age 65 or earlier. Should you decide to retire early, you will receive a reduced pension.

In either case, it is important to apply at least six months before retirement or you may lose some initial payments.

It is very important that you periodically (every year or two) check that the Record of Earnings, on which your pension will be based, is correct. The Record of Earnings is the governments record of your contributions to the Canada Pension Plan. If you have not received a statement in the last two years, you may do so through the offices indicated below.

Spouses who have both reached age 60 may share their CPP retirement pensions. This would be beneficial if one spouse is in a higher tax bracket than the other. Retirement pensions under the CPP may not be shared.

Where To Apply For Canada Pension

Information and application forms for the Canada Pension Plan, which operates throughout Canada, (except in Quebec, which has its own plan) may be obtained through the Income Security Programs, Client Service Centers. There are offices across Canada.

Documents Needed When Applying For Canada Pension

When you apply to receive Canada Pension (and likely any other benefit package from the government), you will need to supply the following information (where applicable):

a) Social Insurance Numbers for you and your spouse.

b) Birth and/or baptismal certificates.

c) Marriage certificate.

d) Divorce papers.

e) Address of former spouse.

2. Old Age Security (OAS)

This pension is payable to anyone 65 years of age or over who meets the residence requirements. If you have been a resident of Canada for 40 years since your 18th birthday, you are eligible for Old Age Security benefits when you reach 65.

At present, the pension is $340.07 a month and could go as high as 713.13 a month, depending on your financial situation. If you have lived in Canada for at least ten years since you wore 18, you are entitled to receive partial benefits. Again, it is wise to apply six months prior to reaching age sixty-five.

For persons with higher-income pensions receiving OAS is subject to a special tax. By 1991, Those with incomes between $50,000 and $75,000 will repay the government a portion of their OAS.

Where To Apply For OAS

The OAS is administered across Canada through the office of the department of Health and Welfare.

The OAS Identification Card (received automatically) may be used when cashing OAS cheques and to receive discounts and privileges from various merchants across Canada. There are a number of benefits, in addition to the Old Age Security Pension, that you may want to investigate. These include:

- Guaranteed Income Supplement (GIS)

- Spouses Allowance

- Extended Spouses Allowance

- Widowed Spouses Allowance

3. Other Programs

Under certain conditions, you may also want to be aware of the following:

- War Veterans Allowance (contact Veterans Affairs Canada)

- Veterans Independence Program (for veterans with special needs)

- Unemployment Insurance Benefit(a lump sum payment may be available at age 65. Apply through any Canada Employment Center)

b) Provincial

Benefits and services offered by each province tend to vary greatly. The list that follows is based on the services found in different Provinces.

Not all Provinces are included in this section, as some have not responded to our request for information. If you require assistance and your Province has not been mentioned, then contact your Provincial offices and ask for departments which offer particular help for seniors.

PRINCE EDWARD ISLAND

1. Health

All residents are covered for hospitalization and medical care without any premium. The rehabilitation Division of the Department of Health and Social Services supplies prosthetics, wheelchairs and hospital beds at no charge. The unit in Charlottetown provides free physiotherapy. Drugs are provided on a needs basis to those receiving Old Age Security (if not full payment, then at cost price through a provincially operated pharmacy). For further information, call 368-4980 (Charlottetown) or contact one of the regional offices.

2. Accommodation

There are a number of programs to assist home owners and renters to maintain and adapt their homes. Some Senior Citizen Housing projects, rural and urban, have rental fees set according to income. Information may be obtained from the Housing Corporation in Charlottetown.

3. Financial Assistance

Provincial Social Assistance will not supplement the Old Age

Security except in special circumstances relating to health, as noted above. Other possible sources would include Veterans pensions and Unemployment Insurance.

NOVA SCOTIA

1. Health Insurance Plan

There is a Pharmacare plan for residents aged 65 years and over who have been registered under the Medical Services Insurance program 429-9700 (Halifax) or (Toll free) 1-429-8880. The Pharmacare card must be applied for when you reach age 65. With this card, Seniors may obtain free prescription drugs.

2. Property Tax Rebate

To qualify, an applicant must be receiving Spouses Allowance or the Guaranteed Income Supplement in January of the year of application and be residing in , and the registered owner of the home.

3. Rental Assistance

This program provides a monthly rebate to assist Senior Citizens who rent on the private market. An applicant must be receiving the Guaranteed Income Supplement to Old Age Security, Spouses Allowance or have a certain yearly income ceiling and be paying a specified percentage of that income on rent.

4. Seniors Special Assistance

A once a year payment to all Seniors receiving the Guaranteed Income Supplement to Old Age Security is available in March of the year of application. Applications are automatically forwarded to eligible Seniors. For further information on this or other programs indicated above, contact the Department of Social Services in Halifax at 424-4500 or any of the regional offices.

5. Housing

The Nova Scotia Department of Housing has a small loans assistance program, a Senior Citizens Public Housing program, a Senior Citizens Assistance program, a Provincial Housing Emergency Repair Program and is involved in Non-Profit Housing projects. Further information may be obtained from the regional offices. There are also Homes For Special Care for disabled Senior Citizens who are unable to remain in their own homes, even with community support services. For information, call the local municipal services or 424-4277 (Halifax).

ONTARIO

1. Senior Citizens Privilege Card

This card can be used for drug benefits under certain circumstances. You should receive this card following your sixty-fifth birthday. For inquiries regarding drug benefits, call 965-9451.

2. Gains Benefit

This is related to the Guaranteed Income Supplement and is calculated automatically, if you are receiving GIS. For information, call 965-8470.

3. Property Tax Grant/Sales Tax Grant

Application forms for these benefits should be received automatically by recipients of Old Age Security. For additional information, call 965-8470.

4. Financial Assistance

Residents requiring immediate financial aid should contact 392-8623 for General Welfare Assistance. For seniors not receiving OAS, women over 60 living alone, seniors supporting dependents, contact 965-1433 for Family Benefits Assistance.

5. Other Benefits And Services

There are many benefits and services provided for Seniors in the area of transportation. Many local and provincial transit systems offer reduced fares for Senior Citizens. In addition, there are special services for disabled Seniors. In Ontario, the following are available:

- Toronto Transit Card for reduced fares.
  Call 392-8701.

- Wheel Trans for the disabled. Call 393-4111.

- Via Rail Services. Call 366-8411.

- Go Transit Services. Call 630-3933.

- Ontario Northland Railway. Call 965-4268.

Information detailing services for Seniors is listed in the booklet, "Senior Wise", available free of charge, from the Provincial Government, Queens Park, Toronto.

MANITOBA

1. Health Services Commission Plan

All residents are covered by the health insurance plan. For further details regarding registration and coverage, call (collect) 786-7101 (Winnipeg).

2. Social Allowance Health Services

This service provides financial assistance for basic drug, dental and optical supplies and other services not covered by the health insurance plan. For eligibility information and assistance, call 944-3744 (Winipeg) or (Toll free) 1-800-282-8060.

3. Tax Assistance

There are a number of tax assistance programs for Senior Citizens. These include: Manitoba Property Tax Credit, Pensioners School Tax Assistance Credit for Home Owners, Cost of Living Tax Credit. For information, applications and assistance, call 943-3401 (Winnipeg).

4. Supplement For Seniors

This program applies to eligible Seniors who are either 55 to 65 or 65 and over. Application is necessary. Call 945-2686 (Winnipeg) or contact your nearest Community Services office. There are many other plans and programs available to the citizens of Manitoba and information is obtainable from various government departments.

ALBERTA

1. Health Care Insurance Plan

Persons 65 and older, their spouses and dependents, are not required to pay premiums for health insurance. Those already registered with the Plan are sent a Proof of Age questionnaire prior to their 65th birthday. Those wishing general information regarding registration and cancellation of Health Care or Blue Cross coverage,should call 427-1432 (Edmonton), 297-6411 (Calgary) or any regional office.

2. Financial Aid For Accommodation

There are a number of programs available to assist the citizens of Alberta. For example:

- Renters Grant, available to those 65 or older who meet the guidelines. Applications are available at Treasury Branches, local city halls or local information centers, or by calling 427-4873 (Edmonton). This program also applies to Mobile Home owners and may be applied for on the Renters Grant form.

- Property Tax Reduction Benefits of up to $1,000, or your total tax bill, is available for those who are eligible. Application forms are available at your municipal tax office.

- Home Heating Protection Program pays a rebate of

$100 for each calendar year, to eligible seniors. These applications are also available at the local municipal taxation office.

3. Financial Assistance

- The Assured Income Plan is related to the Guaranteed Income Supplement and is calculated automatically, if you receive GIS. For information, call 427-7286 (Edmonton).

- Social Allowance provides financial help in meeting basic needs. For information, contact the local office of the Alberta Social Services which is listed under Government of Alberta in the telephone directory.

- The Widow's Pension Program provides financial assistance to widows or widowers, age 55 and over but under 65, who have limited or no income. For information, call 422-4080 (Edmonton).

BRITISH COLUMBIA

1. The Medical Services Plan

An eligible Senior Citizen, prior to turning 65, should receive a Plan A card automatically. This plan provides assistance to permanent residents who are 65 years of age or older. Benefits include reduced dispensing and drug costs. For information, call 387-3724 (Victoria) or Zenith 2179 or 681-9171 toll-free from the Lower Mainland.

2. Guaranteed Available Income for Need (GAIN)

GAIN for Senior Citizens is a monthly payment by the provincial government to ensure a guaranteed minimum income level for residents receiving Federal Old Age Security and Guaranteed Income Supplement or Federal Spouses' Allowance. If eligibility exists, payments can commence at age 60. No application is necessary. For further information, call 387-4331 (Victoria), 682-0391 (Vancouver) or, toll-free, Zenith 2656.

3. Taxable Income Deductions

The Old Age Exemption and the Pension Income Deduction allow Senior Citizens to deduct from income when calculating taxable income. The Land Tax Deferment Act allows deferment of property taxes on the principal residence until the death of the applicant or transfer of property. For additional information, contact the Ministry of Finance and Corporate Relations.

4. Housing Services

A Home Owner Grant reduces school and municipal taxation for eligible Senior Citizens. Contact the Ministry of Municipal Affairs.

Eligible Senior Citizens may also obtain cash assistance for rental expenses and apply for subsidized and affordable housing (in the Lower Mainland) through the Ministry of Social Services and Housing/B.C. Housing Management Commission 433-1711 in Vancouver.

c) Local Municipalities

In most communities across Canada, there are private, non-profit and municipal agencies that will provide information and help to Senior Citizens. In large metropolitan areas, contact the offices of the Provincial Government. In Ontario, contact Seniors' Information Service at the offices of the Ministry of Community and Social Services, or obtain the Guide for Senior Citizens Services and Programs from the Minister for Senior Citizens' Affairs.

In smaller communities, contact the local municipal offices for information and direction. Frequently, local banks and business organizations honour Senior Citizens by providing free or reduced rate banking services and discounted purchases.

More Blessed To Give Than Receive

40

Giving is a natural expression of love. When we love someone, we want to be with them and share our time, emotions, dreams, goals, success, and provide for their needs. Actions truly do speak louder than words.

The Bible has numerous references concerning giving which allows us to arrive at certain principles. These principles are relevant today, regardless of our financial situation.

1. Attitude is critical. Our willingness to give cheerfully is more important than the amount we give. When the apostle Paul was writing to the Corinthian church, he was encouraging them to follow through on their earlier commitments. When he used the word cheerfully, he also meant promptly and graciously. Our attitude towards giving should allow us to give promptly, graciously and cheerfully.

The amount of money we give is not important when compared to the attitude behind the gift. "Many rich people threw in large amounts. But a poor widow came and put in two very small copper coins, worth only a fraction of a penny." (Mk12:41,42)

When Jesus was teaching His disciples, He used this example to illustrate the attitude of a joyous heart willing to give in aid of others.

Jesus continued to teach His disciples when He said, "I tell you the truth, this poor widow has put more into the treasury than all the others. They all gave out of their wealth; but she, out of her poverty, put in everything - all she had to live on." (Mk.12:43,44)

While this example shows the widow giving 100 percent, statistics in Canada indicates that the Christian community gives approximately one percent of their income to charity.

2. We must strive to fulfil our financial commitments.

3. Give to others who are in need, and they will help you in your time of need. This is a basic principle of reciprocity. This principle helps ensure that each will have as much as they need.

4. Motive is important. We should give for the pleasure and joy of giving to Jesus Christ and not for what we can get back for ourselves.

How much should I give?

1. Each of us should fulfil any previous promises.

2. Each of us needs to make up our own mind on the matter of giving. "Whoever sows sparingly, will also reap sparingly, and whoever sows generously will also reap generously." (2Co.9:6)

3. Each person should give in proportion to what God has given them. "Each man should give what he has decided in his heart to give, not reluctantly nor under compulsion."(2Co.9:7)

4. God gives to us so we can give to others. "You will be made rich in every way so that you can be generous on every occasion and through us your generosity will result in thanksgiving to God."(2Co.9:10,11)

5. Sacrificial giving must be responsible. While Paul encourages giving he does not suggest we should be giving to the point that those who depend upon us

must do without. He does not mean that those who receive your gifts should have an easy time at your expense. (2Co.8:13)

God Is The Provider Of All

Everything we have and call ours, has come from the hand of God. He is the Creator and through His grace we have received a multitude of blessings.

The earth is the Lord's and everything in it, the world, and all who live in it. (Ps.24:1) And in Psalm 89:11 we read, "The heavens are yours, and yours also the earth; you founded the world and all that is in it."

In James 1:17 we read,

"Every good and perfect gift is from above, coming down from the Father of the heavenly lights, who does not change like shifting shadows. He chose to give us birth through the word of truth."

Acknowledging God as the Creator, we realize that His supply has no limits. God is in charge of our finances and can provide help in times of need. Although we may have confidence in our ability to solve our own problems, we are no match for God.

"You may say to yourself, My power and the strength of my hands have produced this wealth for me. But remember the Lord your God for it is He who gives you the ability to produce wealth, and so confirms His covenant." (Dt.8:17,18)

We Make Use Of His Gifts

While God supplies our needs, it is our responsibility to wisely use the gifts, talents and resources He provides.

It is God's intention to multiply our resources. "I have planted the seed, Apollos water it, but God made it grow. So neither he who plants nor he who waters is anything, but only God, who makes things grow." (1Co.3:6,7)

If we are diligent and careful with the things entrusted to our care, God will cause those talents and other resources to grow. As we increase in wealth, we are able to help others even more. This includes our family, church, and para church organizations.

As Christians who will one day stand before God, our heart's cry is to hear Him say..."Well done, good and faithful servant! You have been faithful with a few things; I will put you in charge of many things. Come share in your Master's happiness!"

Multiplying His Provisions

The example from Jesus' parable of the talents in Matthew 25 and Luke 19, is quite clear. We are to make use of our talents, money and other resources, or we lose them. As we exercise wisdom and understanding we gain success. God's purpose for increasing our resources is to allow us the privilege of helping others in need. In 2Co.8:4, Paul notes that the Macedonian church "urgently pleaded with us for the privilege of sharing in this service to the saints." How did they come to a point in their lives where they pleaded for an opportunity to give? In verse 5 Paul notes, " And they did not do as we expected, but they gave themselves first to the Lord and then to us in keeping with God's will." They made God their number one priority. They put Him first and everything else followed. How often the Bible makes this very important point. As Jesus instructs in Matthew 6:33, "Seek first the kingdom of God." He must come first in every area of our lives."

It is not difficult for God to multiply our resources. Jesus lived out clear examples of God's ability to increase His blessings and how the increase was to be used. After Jesus spent several hours teaching, the disciples reminded Him that the crowds were becoming hungry.

> *"How many loaves do you have? Jesus asked." When He heard there were only seven loaves and one fish to feed a crowd of four thousand hungry people, He instructed them to sit down on the ground. "Then He took the seven loaves and the fish, and when He had*

given thanks, He broke them and gave them to His
disciples, and they in turn to the people. They all ate
and were satisfied." (Mt15:33-37)

If we allow God to use us as a channel for His blessings, He will multiply our giving, increase our joy and provide for our needs as He promised. (Ph.4:19)

"But just as you excel in everything—in faith, in speech,
in knowledge, in complete earnestness and in your love
for us—see that you also excel in this grace of giving. I am
not commanding you, but I want to test the sincerity of
your love by comparing it with the earnestness of others."
(2Co.8:7,8)

Charity Begins At Home

41

One would suspect that Christians, who recognize that all their wealth comes from God, would also be more willing to share this wealth than would non-Christians. While statistics prove this to be the case, they also show that Christians could probably afford to be more generous.

Latest figures indicate that while Canadians on average give approximately 0.053% of their taxable income to worthy causes, Christians give away only 2% of their income. This is in spite of the fact that the government is quite willing to use the tax system to encourage all Canadians to give more of their money away. As individuals increase the size of gifts to charitable causes, the government will ensure that income tax time is a little easier to take.

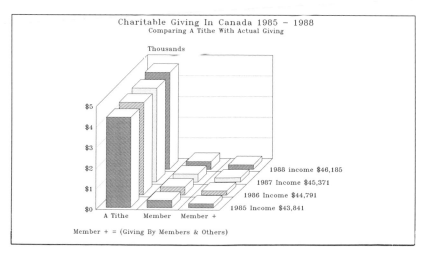

Charitable Giving In Canada 1985 – 1988
Comparing A Tithe With Actual Giving

Thousands

1988 income $46,185
1987 Income $45,371
1986 Income $44,791
1985 Income $43,841

A Tithe   Member   Member +

Member + = (Giving By Members & Others)

Up until 1987, the government allowed Canadians to deduct their charitable giving (which includes offerings to churches) from their total income. Beginning with the 1988 income tax returns, Ottawa moved to a series of tax credits for most deductions. While this system has been unfair in some cases, for the purposes of charitable giving, it has enabled many Canadians to receive higher refunds or decrease the amount of tax payable.

Under this new system, the first $250 of total charitable giving allows you to claim a 17% federal tax credit. When provincial tax is taken into consideration, the total credit increases to 27%. Donations above $250, allows you to claim a federal tax credit of 29%, a figure that jumps to 45% when provincial tax is added.

While it is human nature to argue that we don't have enough money to give to others, the income tax system ensures that lower income Canadians can in fact increase their tax refund by giving donations to charity under the new tax system. For Canadians having less than $55,600 in taxable income, donations exceeding $250 ensures that their tax credit is worth far more than it was under the old system of deductions.

Canadians in the top tax bracket who have more than $55,600 in taxable income, are not penalized under the new system. All of their donations over $250 receive the same type of treatment as if they were deductions. Therefore, there is no change for them under the new system, compared with the old method of calculating tax.

There are a number of other ways to increase your tax benefits under the Income Tax Act. Following are the most common:

1. Once you donate over $250 in one year, make extra donations in December instead of putting it off to the first few months of the next year. This will ensure that your tax savings will be realized one year earlier.

2. Your total claim for donations can not exceed 20% of your net income in one year. However, if you donate more than 20% in one year, you can submit a claim

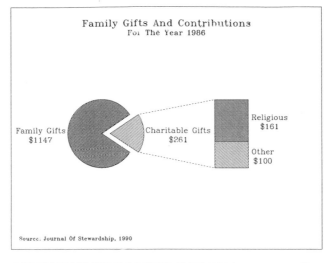

Family Gifts And Contributions
For The Year 1986

Family Gifts
$1147

Charitable Gifts
$261

Religious
$161

Other
$100

Source. Journal Of Stewardship, 1990

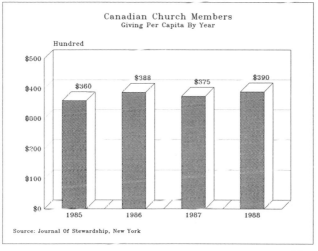

Canadian Church Members
Giving Per Capita By Year

Hundred

$500

$400

$300

$200

$100

$0

1985	1986	1987	1988
$360	$388	$375	$390

Source: Journal Of Stewardship, New York

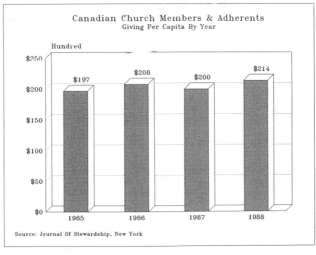

Canadian Church Members & Adherents
Giving Per Capita By Year

Hundred

$250

$200

$150

$100

$50

$0

1985	1986	1987	1988
$197	$208	$200	$214

Source: Journal Of Stewardship, New York

135

and have the excess applied to your taxes during the next five years.

3. If you donate less than $250 every year for two or more years, you should consider combining the donations and claiming them on one year's return. In this way, you can increase your tax savings if your total donations over several years exceeds $250.

4. While married couples often claim donations separately on their tax returns, it could save you money if you combine your donations on one return. If your total donations are over $250, this will ensure higher savings.

A friend of mine once remarked that for a number of years he refused to claim his charitable donations when filling out his income tax return. He argued that it was nobody's business how much he gave to charities and backed up his statement with the quote that we should not let our left hand know what our right hand is doing. He also felt that claiming donations on his income tax was boastful and in fact bordered on pride.

My friend was not alone in this argument. I have heard a number of people use this reasoning over the years. However, in not claiming your charitable donations or church tithes, we can be displaying a lack of stewardship. If we claim our donations, the government takes this into consideration and allows us to either decrease our taxes or increase the size of our tax refund.

My friend now claims all of his donations and as a result has increased the size of his tax refund in recent years. He now puts this larger refund to good use by turning around and donating the increased amount to various charitable organizations.

He remarked to me recently that he compares the relationship between increased donations to charity and a higher tax refund, with Canadian Tire money. Just like Canadian Tire money, even when you use it, you always receive more. The cycle never ends.

Review
Investments

42

Yesterday's Investments Could Cost You Money

What could have been a wise investment last year, may not be such a wise investment today. Investments change over time. The ultimate responsibility for the success or failure of an investment program must rest with each investor. Often, someone will make an investment and feel that because they have studied the marketplace, they can now forget their decision and wait for the mail man to deliver their dividend check.

Following are some points for consideration to help you keep track of your investments and to monitor their achievements:

- Always investigate then invest.

- Ask questions from people who have a proven track record of success.

- Conduct additional research in the area of your investment.

- Don't keep an investment forever.

- Don't panic if there is a sudden market shift in your investment area.

- Never buy on a hot tip or a rumour regardless of how high the profit may be.

- Remember to also invest where neither moth nor rust can destroy your investment.

- Review your investment portfolio on a regular basis, either semi-annually or annually.

- Seek professional help.

- Stay in touch with your investment counsellor.

View your return on investment in percentage points and not dollars. A penny stock that goes from 10 cents to 20 cents provides a 100% profit. When was the last time your bank paid you 100% interest?

Watch for changes in tax regulations which might affect your investment.

Watch changes in the Canadian economy and how these changes might affect the value of your investment.

You will never go broke taking a profit, no matter know small the rate. Again, look at the capital gains in percentage terms.

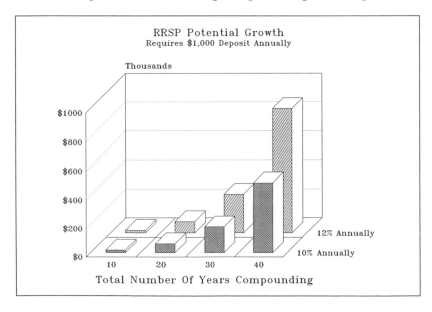

Collapsing Your RRSP

43

If you live long enough, and most people do, you will have to decide what to do with the proceeds from your RRSP. Presently, your RRSP matures by the end of the calendar year you turn 71. The choices are not that complicated and are limited to three possible options.

1. Collapse the RRSP and pay the tax owing on the full amount. If you have held your RRSP for any period of time, your pension and other income, combined with your RRSP, would likely move you into the highest tax bracket. The net result is that you end up paying more tax. This is not the best idea.

2. Purchase an annuity from your insurance agent. Your RRSP proceeds move directly into the annuity without attracting any tax. You will receive a payment every month and will be taxed on only the amount of the payment.

It is important to note that when you buy an annuity the money is locked in. You have, in fact, exchanged your money for a monthly income. Although this money can not be refunded if you change your mind, this may not necessarily be bad. For example, if you locked in at a time when interest rates are high, you benefit for the term of the annuity. On the other hand, if interest rates were low, you are receiving a smaller monthly income benefit.

There are three basic types of annuities you can purchase:

(a) A Life term annuity provides a secure income for life. It guarantees payments for various terms, such as 5, 10, 15 or 20 years.

(b) You might want to consider a Fixed Term annuity which provides guaranteed payments for a fixed number of years. This annuity terminates at age 90 and typical terms would be 5, 10 or 20 years. If you die before reaching 90, a beneficiary, named by you, will receive the payments for the remaining term.

(c) If you are comfortable with investments, a Variable Annuity might interest you. This type of annuity, also called a segregated fund, provides payments which vary according to the performance of the special fund.

3. A third choice is to purchase a RRIF (Registered Retirement Income Fund). A RRIF operates similar to an annuity in that it makes regular monthly payment to you. The major difference between an annuity and a RRIF is that a RRIF is more flexible. The payments from a RRIF often increase over time to offset the rising cost of inflation.

Like a self-directed RRSP, a RRIF allows you to decide whether your money is invested in, for example, mortgage funds or balanced mutual funds. You still have control over the funds, but you must withdraw at least the minimum required by law.

The following is a formula showing how much money you must withdraw each year. This example is based on a 70-year-old:

90 (age RRIF is collapsed) - Present Age (70) = 20

In the first year, 1/20th of the fund must be withdrawn.

The next year, 1/19th of the fund must be withdrawn and so on.

RRSP Or Mortgage: Everything Is Not Created Equal

Many home owners struggle with the question of whether to put extra money into their RRSP or pay down their mortgage. This is the question I have been asked more than any other, regardless of which province I visit. The short answer to this question is that it depends upon the circumstances of each family.

First of all, you must consider the life style and goals you and your spouse have established. For some Canadians, their house is looked upon as a future source of retirement income. They plan to sell the house and invest the proceeds, living off the interest or income. The potential difficulty with this scenario is that we seldom receive the amount we expect from the sale. We must remember that there are closing expenses, moving expenses, and since we need to live somewhere, money to pay for other accommodation.

On the other hand, paying off the mortgage can ease the pressure on our monthly cash flow. Money which would have gone to the mortgage company can be re-directed to an RRSP. Since the limit on RRSP contributions is being raised from the present level of $7,500 to $11,500 in 1991, with a limit of 18% of earned income, you will be able to place more money into this retirement plan.

Remember, both sources of investment receive special tax treatment. When you sell you home, if it is your principal residence, you are not taxed while your RRSP contributions are not taxed until the funds are withdrawn.

Some people seek the best of both worlds by placing their extra cash into an RRSP, refund it in the spring and then apply this money to their mortgage.

Some brief calculations (you will need an amortization schedule) can help you determine which choice offers the greatest financial gain. First, determine the amount of money you have to invest, examine the amortization schedule and calculate how much money is saved by prepaying your mortgage. (You can do your own calculations or have your mortgage company provide the figures.)

Next, determine how much money you would earn from an RRSP, using the same amount of money you have available for investment purposes. (You can acquire this information from companies selling RRSP's or you can find the information in brochures published by various companies.)

A comparison of your answers should help guide your decision. During your decision, consider your attitude about investments, your present level of cash flow, as well as the present or future demands on your funds. Do you need security or are you the type of person willing to take a risk? These are important considerations for you and your spouse to review in determining what is best for you.

```
PRINCIPAL          : $  116,925.00   COMPOUNDED  SEMI-ANNUALLY
INTEREST RATE      :       12.000%
YEARS OF AMORTIZATION:       25      STARTING DATE      :  JANUARY 01, 1991.
INTEREST FACTOR    : 0.0097587942    FIRST PAYMENT DUE  :  FEBRUARY 01, 1991.
MONTHLY PAYMENT    : $    1206.55
```

#	DUE DATE	INTEREST	PRINCIPAL	BALANCE OF LOAN
1	FEBRUARY 01, 1991.	1,141.05	65.50	$ 116,859.50
2	MARCH 01, 1991.	1,140.41	66.14	$ 116,793.36
3	APRIL 01, 1991.	1,139.76	66.79	$ 116,726.57
4	MAY 01, 1991.	1,139.11	67.44	$ 116,659.13
5	JUNE 01, 1991.	1,138.45	68.10	$ 116,591.03
6	JULY 01, 1991.	1,137.79	68.76	$ 116,522.27
7	AUGUST 01, 1991.	1,137.12	69.43	$ 116,452.84
8	SEPTEMBER 01, 1991.	1,136.44	70.11	$ 116,382.73
9	OCTOBER 01, 1991.	1,135.76	70.79	$ 116,311.94
10	NOVEMBER 01, 1991.	1,135.06	71.49	$ 116,240.45
11	DECEMBER 01, 1991.	1,134.37	72.18	$ 116,168.27
12	JANUARY 01, 1992.	1,133.66	72.89	$ 116,095.38
13	FEBRUARY 01, 1992.	1,132.95	73.60	$ 116,021.78
14	MARCH 01, 1992.	1,132.23	74.32	$ 115,947.46
15	APRIL 01, 1992.	1,131.51	75.04	$ 115,872.42
16	MAY 01, 1992.	1,130.78	75.77	$ 115,796.65
17	JUNE 01, 1992.	1,130.04	76.51	$ 115,720.14
18	JULY 01, 1992.	1,129.29	77.26	$ 115,642.88
19	AUGUST 01, 1992.	1,128.54	78.01	$ 115,564.87
20	SEPTEMBER 01, 1992.	1,127.77	78.78	$ 115,486.09
21	OCTOBER 01, 1992.	1,127.00	79.55	$ 115,406.54
22	NOVEMBER 01, 1992.	1,126.23	80.32	$ 115,326.22
23	DECEMBER 01, 1992.	1,125.44	81.11	$ 115,245.11
24	JANUARY 01, 1993.	1,124.65	81.90	$ 115,163.21
25	FEBRUARY 01, 1993.	1,123.85	82.70	$ 115,080.51
26	MARCH 01, 1993.	1,123.05	83.50	$ 114,997.01
27	APRIL 01, 1993.	1,122.23	84.32	$ 114,912.69
28	MAY 01, 1993.	1,121.41	85.14	$ 114,827.55
29	JUNE 01, 1993.	1,120.58	85.97	$ 114,741.58
30	JULY 01, 1993.	1,119.74	86.81	$ 114,654.77
31	AUGUST 01, 1993.	1,118.89	87.66	$ 114,567.11
32	SEPTEMBER 01, 1993.	1,118.04	88.51	$ 114,478.60
33	OCTOBER 01, 1993.	1,117.17	89.38	$ 114,389.22
34	NOVEMBER 01, 1993.	1,116.30	90.25	$ 114,298.97
35	DECEMBER 01, 1993.	1,115.42	91.13	$ 114,207.84
36	JANUARY 01, 1994.	1,114.53	92.02	$ 114,115.82

```
FINAL PAYMENT (BAL + P + I) due on FEBRUARY 01, 1994. : $ 115,322.37
PRINCIPAL PAID   : $  116,925.00   INTEREST PAID   : $  40,626.62
```

Source: Kissystems, Scarboro, On.

142

Starting A Small Business

If you become involved in a small business, you are permitted to deduct the expenses you incur in the process. The rules have changed recently if you operate a business from home, but you can still deduct some house expenses if you qualify.

Let's examine some of the expenses and capital cost allowances (fancy words for depreciation) the small business owner can deduct. Be sure to keep an accurate record of all receipts, so you may support your claims. While some people still use shoe boxes to store their receipts, file folders are easier to find should the tax man pay a visit.

Accounting Fees	Office Supplies
Bank Charges	Office Expenditures
Equipment	Auto Expenses
Telephone Expenses	Advertising & Promotion
Postage	Furniture & Fixtures
Magazine Subscriptions	Letterhead & Business
Books	Seminar Fees
Professional Affiliations	Parking Expenses
Public Transportation	Taxicabs
Auto Maintenance	Utility Expenses

Interest Charges	Business Development Expenses
Staffing	Computers & Software
Business Meals (80% Deductible)	Cards

Some of the less obvious deductions you might claim, as part of your business expenses, could include:

| Garden Services | Snow Ploughing |
| Lighting | Minor Repairs |

An accountant is very helpful in this area. I strongly encourage you to seek the advice of one when operating any business.

The Home Office

46

If you operate a small business from your home and it qualifies as a home office with Revenue Canada, we have good news for you. You can deduct a portion of your on-going home expenses from your business income.

All deductions are based on a percentage of the total area occupied by your business and by your family. Based on the percentage of usage, you may deduct:

Rent   Repairs

Interest on your mortgage   Household Utilities

Property Taxes   Maintenance

Insurance

Your home must be the primary place of business. This is where you meet clients, conduct meetings, etc. You are not allowed another office elsewhere, although a client could provide you with some office space.

Be careful when deciding to deduct capital cost allowance (CCA). When you do deduct CCA, such as depreciation on your house, Revenue Canada considers a portion to be related to your business. When you sell the house, that portion of the selling price is not considered tax free revenue. In fact, it is added to your income. If you are a high income earner, you may pay the maximum rate of tax on that portion. Best to discuss this with your accountant.

Remember, you can only claim your expenses against the income you earn from your business in that location.

As a Christian business person, we must be honest and above reproach. We should be the standard by which others will be measured. We must have the right attitude and operate our business with integrity and honesty. There is no substitute. God weighs our motives.

"We must give to Caesar, what is Caesar's and to God what is God's." (Mt. 22:21)

What Is Power Of Attorney?

47

What Is Power Of Attorney?

This is a legal procedure whereby you give someone else control over your affairs when you are absent or unable to manage for yourself.

This is a binding document and should be prepared by a lawyer. Careful thought must be given to the seriousness of giving someone else either complete or partial control over your affairs.

A power of attorney has many benefits. In the event that you are incapacitated by illness, someone appointed by you has the power to carry out your wishes or provide for your care. If you have a family, you are assured that they will receive an uninterrupted cash flow.

A power of attorney can be limited and apply only to a certain area. For example, you could give power of attorney to a relative authorizing them to sell your home. Once the sale is completed and the proceeds given to you, the power of attorney would cease.

 Failure to provide someone with the power of attorney, can lead to serious complications if you are incapacitated. In this case, a court order would have to be obtained in order to secure the necessary funds to pay for your care. This procedure can be a lengthy and costly affair.

If an individual had given significant amounts of money to charitable causes during their lifetime, this would cease if they had failed to invest someone with power of attorney authority. On the other hand, by appointing someone, you could ensure that your wishes would be respected in that your favourite charities would still receive your donations.

By appointing someone you trust to carry out your wishes if you bocome incapacitated, you can ensure that all your wishes are carried out as you instruct. This might not be the case if the courts were to appoint someone to look after your estate.

Financial
Independence
For Widows
And Widowers

48

Financial Independence

A spouse's death is one of the most traumatic experiences a married person will ever face. Not only does the remaining spouse experience grief, but often faces financial difficulty at the same time. This problem is more pronounced when the surviving spouse is older and perhaps unable to find employment.

Advance planning is the key to success. However, that may not be possible in all situations. The following possible sources of income may help alleviate some of the financial pressures for widows and widowers.

1. Life Insurance Policies

2. Company Pension Plans

3. Annuity Income

4. RRSP's

5. RRIF's

6. Canada Pension Plan Survivor Benefits, Old Age Security, Guaranteed Income Supplement.

7. Benefits from the Federal Department of Veterans Affairs are available to Canada's war veterans and

former members of the Peacetime Armed Forces. The benefits include disability pensions, financial assistance under the War Veterans Allowance, medical expenses, dental care, eye glasses as well as additional benefits. For details, you should contact the Department of Veterans Affairs.

8. If you are employable, consider part-time or full-time employment

9. Securities, Bonds, Canada Savings Bonds

10. Selling family assets such as cottages, second cars, or family home.

11. Renting space in your home or sharing an apartment to reduce rent.

12. Property Tax Rebate programs provide a partial refund of your property taxes. Contact your provincial government for details.

Living On A Fixed Income

Most of us recognize it is not easy living on a fixed pension. In fact, in some cases the title might better read surviving on a fixed pension. It is for this reason, I recommend beginning a retirement program as early as possible.

Although many seniors may be on a fixed income, they can improve their standard of living. Most seniors, at the time of writing this book, have experienced the hardships of the thirties and forties. They were creative, hard working and have proved to be a source of knowledge and wisdon when needed.

Remember how the "grey power" dealt with Ottawa in the 80's and the impact they had on the government. Canadian seniors are creative and they can increase their income through their creative ideas. Here are a few suggestions for increasing income for seniors on a fixed pension.

- Be sure you are receiving all the benefits allowed by our governments,

- Review existing investments regularly,

- Consider baby-sitting,

- Consider house-sitting while neighbours are on vacation,

- If your health permits, consider part-time employment,

- Begin a mail order business,

- Make toys for Christmas gifts and sell to friends,

- Become a teacher or part-time consultant in your area of lifetime employment,

- Consider renting your home to a major company for the winter months. Your home could be used for out-of-town executives visiting the company. Charge the going rate and move to less expensive accommodation in Florida for the winter, and

- Consider renting a room to a student. They could use a quiet place to study and the company would be good for you.

Applying For Canada Pension Death Benefits

49

A Canada Pension Death Benefit is payable to the survivor when a spouse or family member dies. The size of the benefit will depend upon the amount of money paid into the Canadian Pension Plan and the length of time the deceased paid into the plan.

You should check with your local government offices to request information and application forms for registering a claim. A certain amount of paper work is required before a claim can be paid. You will need the following documents:

1. Social Insurance numbers of the deceased and surviving spouse.

2. Birth or Baptismal certificate of the deceased and surviving spouse.

3. Death Certificate from either the attending doctor or funeral director.

4. Marriage Certificate

If the deceased was receiving a pension check from the government, they need to be notified of the death. These benefits cease at the end of the month in which the death occurs. If a check arrives after the death, it should be returned to the office of issue and they will re-issue a replacement check payable to the next of kin or estate. If the spouses held a joint account, then the surviving spouse may deposit the check.

Life Insurance Claims

A copy of any life insurance policy should be reviewed and the agent or insurance company notified of the death. The insurance company will require a death certificate to process a claim. Should the deceased be employed at the time of death, the personnel department should be notified immediately.

Proceeds from insurance policies are not taxable income and should not be reported on a tax return.

A Glimpse
At GST

50

The Goods and Services Tax was passed by the House of Commons on April 10, 1990 for implementation January 1,1991. The GST rate is expected to be 7%, a reduction from the initial proposal of 9% and the federal tax system will terminate when GST begins.

The highlights as it applies to the consumer.

- 7% is applied to most goods and services sold to the consumer for domestic use.

- Establishing a system of tax credits to reduce the effect of tax on tax as goods flow through the economy.

- Some goods and services maybe partially exempted from the tax.

- Goods for export will not be subject to the GST.

Apart from an increase in our inflation rate the GST will lower prices of some goods and services. Presently the federal sales tax of 13.5% will be removed and replaced by the GST at the point of sale.

Some present items such as cars, which disclose the present federal sales tax, should have a price decrease. The reason for not decreasing, may evolve around a shifting of the present tax to a marketing or other related expense. It is reasonable to expect that the competitive forces may cause the prices to be reduced.

GST will not apply to tax-exempt goods and services. Tax-exempt goods and services will not be subject to, or partici-pate in the tax credit program relating to GST.

Tax-Exempt Items

- day care services;
- legal aid services;
- eductational services;
- long-term residential rents
- resale housing, including personal use property such as cottages and hobby farms;
- health and dental services, including hospital and nursing home services;
- goods and services provided by charities;
- most domestic financial services;
- goods or services provided by non-profit organiza-tions, public-sector orginizations and governments.

Zero-Rated Items

Zero-rated items allow a tax credit for taxes paid when the consumer is not charged GST. Such items include

- prescription drugs;
- medical devices
- groceries
- agricultural and fishery products;
- exports;
- prescribed major farm and fishing equipment pur-chases; and

- rental of farm land under a sharecropping arrangement between registrants.

In the case of a company, in order to claim GST credits, a company will need to be registered under the GST program.

SPECIFIC INDUSTRIES

Housing

Resale housing is considered used-housing and will not be subject to GST. New construction is subject to the GST, if the closing date is after January 1, 1991.

There will be a rebate given on new housing subject to the GST. The rebate will be 36% of the GST paid on a new house selling for $350,000 or less. The rebate is on the tax paid, not the selling price. For houses costing between the $350,000 and $450,000 the rebate will be reduced from the allowable maximum of $8,750.00 by $87.50 for each $1,000 over the $350,000 price tag.

For Example	
New House Price	$275,000.00
GST 7% of house price	$ 19,250.00
GST Rebate 36%	$ 6,930.00

The GST rebate as a percentage of the house cost is approximately 2.52%.

Clothing

Presently, clothing is not subject to GST. Therefore, our clothing costs will likely increase with GST. Buy your winter and summer clothes before December 31,1990 and save some tax dollars.

Automobiles

Automobile include a significant amount of federal sales tax. The price of cars, vans and trucks should decrease.

Funeral Services

Beginning in 1991, funeral services will be subject to GST. Prepaid funerals arranged before September, 1990 will not be subject to GST.

Food

Basic groceries will not be subject to tax. However, basic groceries will not include candies, soft drinks, confections and snack food. In addition, restaurant meals and take-out food will be subject to tax. The following food will be tax-exempt.

- Food services included as part of a basic fee for exempt accommodation (eg., university residence or nursing home);

- meal plans providing all meals for a continuous period of one month or more. (eg., students living off campus who buy a meal plan at the school;

- prepared meals served in a primary or secondary shcool;

- prepared meals supplied by Meals on Wheels or similar programs;

- food and drink supplied by a charity or non-profit organization in the course of relieving poverty, suffering or distress.

There is still much to be resolved in the area of GST. The information contained here was derived from GST Impact, The Final Countdown by Deloitte & Touche. This is a good book and well worth reading.

Glossary Of Terms

Administrator	This is the person appointed by a court to administer and settle the estate of someone who has died without a Will.
Amortization	This is the repayment of a large debt, usually a mortgage, over a specific period of time.
Amortization Schedule	A financial table which illustrates a mortgage repayment by listing the opening balance, the interest paid, the Principal Paid and the closing balance.
Annuity	An agreement between and individual and a financial institution or life insurance company. You provide an amount of money and in exchange the institution promises to provide regular payments to you.
Assets	Anything owned by an individual or a corporation.
Average Daily Balance	This is a method used in calculating the amount of interest you will pay, usually applicable to a credit card, when you do not pay your account in full.
Balance Sheet	A financial statement which shows the net worth, assets and liabilities of an individual or corporation at a particular point in time.
Blended Payments	The repayment of a debt in equal payments of principal and interest on a regular basis for a specific period of time.
Broker	Someone who acts between the buyer and the seller such as a real estate or insurance broker.
Budget	A financial document which indicates income and expenses over a period of time. It is a necessary ingredient for any financial plan.
Cash Surrender Value	The amount of cash received if a particular type of life insurance policy is terminated.

Cash Flow	Cash flow is the amount of money left from your paycheque after deductions. It specifically refers to the amount of income coming in and the amount paid out during a period of time.
Chattel Mortgage	This is property that is used as security for a loan. It is usually items such as cars and boats.
Closing Costs	Closing costs are the extra costs paid to your lawyer at the time of completing a real estate transaction.
Closing Date	A real estate term used to mark the date when the sale of a property becomes final and the new owner takes possession of the house.
Codicil	A codicil is any amendment to an existing Will. It is attached to the Will and can be used to make changes without re-writing a Will.
Collateral	Collateral refers to property pledged by a borrower as security for a loan. If the borrower does not repay the loan, the collateral can be seized by the lender.
Collateral Mortgage	A collateral mortgage is one where the borrower uses the equity in a house or property as security for a mortgage.
Compound Interest	This is the amount of interest, earned or paid, on interest previously earned.
Cost Of Credit	This is the actual cost of borrowing money. By law, it must be disclosed at the time you negotiate a loan.
Credit Rating	A credit rating is how your creditors rate you. It is based on salary, and your promptness in repaying borrowed funds.
Current Asset	A current asset is easily converted into cash and can include bonds, securities, etc.
Debt	An obligation to pay an amount of money to a person or company in the future.
Deferred Annuity	This is an annuity contract where your defer the income until sometime in the future. Normally, you would purchase a deferred annuity when the interest rates are high.
Deferred Gift	A deferred gift occurs in a situation where you provide for a financial gift to be received sometime in the future. Usually it is mentioned in your Will.

Defined Benefit Plan	This is a pension which provides a certain level of income, expressed in either a dollar amount or as a percentage of earnings for each year of service under the plan.
Dividend Tax Credit	This is a tax credit allowed against any income earned from investing in Canadian companies. As a result, income earned through these dividends is taxed at a lower rate.
Equity	Equity is the difference between your assets and your liabilities. Sometimes called Net Worth.
Estate Planning	A process of planning to ensure the maximum dispersement of assets while incurring a minimum of taxation following one's death.
Executor	A person (male) appointed in a Will to settle the financial affairs and other obligations of the deceased.
Executrix	A person (female) appointed in a Will to settle the financial affairs and other obligations of the deceased.
Financial Plan	A process of evaluating present financial status with a view to achieving future financial requirements.
Fixed Assets	Assets which are not easily converted into cash such as buildings, land etc.
Fixed Expenses	These are expenses which occur on a regular basis and do not vary in the amount.
Goals	The task you are trying to accomplish through implementing various financial objectives.
Goods And Services Tax (GST)	The federal tax charged to the consumer at the current rate of 7% beginning January, 1991.
Gross Income	The amount of income earned before any deductions.
Guaranteed Investment Certificates	A certificate issued by a financial institution with a guarantee to pay a predetermined rate of interest for a stipulated period of time.
Guaranteed Income Supplement	An amount of money paid to retired persons with limited income and is not subject to taxation.
Guardian	An individual appointed in a Will to provide on-going care for a minor or individual(s) with "special" needs.

Impulse Buying	Making a purchase without giving prior thought to the particular purchase.
Income Splitting	The process of dividing income among family members so as to pay less tax.
Indexed Annuities	This is an annuity which provides some protection against inflation. This type of annuity can provide for full protection against inflation or a set percentage increase each year.
Inflation	The amount of increase in the cost of living, or the decrease in your purchasing power, usually measured in percentage terms.
Intestate	This term refers to someone who dies without leaving a Will.
Liabilities	Any money owed to an individual or a corporation. A summary of the amounts owing appear on a Balance Sheet.
Long Term Goals	Usually refers to goals which will take longer than one year to accomplish.
Long Term Objectives	Usually objectives which will run longer than one year and are directed toward achieving long term goals.
Marginal Rate	It is the percentage rate of income tax you will pay on the next dollar earned. It is a combination of your provincial and federal tax.
Money Purchase	A plan which provides a pension based on whatever pension income can be purchased at retirement from accumulated contributions and investment earnings in the plan.
Mortgage	A mortgage is a debt payable to a lender.
Mortgage Term	This is the period of time that a set interest rate will be charged. At the end of the term, the interest rate could change.
Mutual Fund	An investment company which combines money from a number of people whose investment goals are similar. The funds are usually invested in a wide variety of securities to provide stability and safety in the event of large price changes in a particular investment.

Net Income	The income remaining after deductions have been taken from total income
Net Worth	This is the difference between what you own and what you owe.
Objectives	The tasks that must be accomplished in order to reach a particular goal.
Per Stirpes	This is a legal term used to make provision for your grandchildren in the event their parents (your children) are deceased. The share of an estate which would go to their parents (your children) passes on to the grandchildren.
Positive Cash Flow	Having more money coming in each period than what is flowing out each period.
Power Of Attorney	A power of attorney is a legal document giving someone else the right to enter in to binding contracts on your behalf. It can be limited to a specific transaction or a general power of attorney allowing someone to represent your interests.
Principal	The amount of money outstanding against a mortgage or loan and is usually repaid with interest over a period of time.
Probate	The process undertaken by which a court attempts to prove the validity of a Will.
RESP	A Registered Education Savings Plan is an income-splitting plan designed to lower taxes of parents or grandparents. There is no tax deduction for contributions but income earned on the contribution accumulates tax free inside the plan.
Retirement Planning	The process of planning for financial security in the retirement years. Ideally, this planning process begins at least ten to twenty years before retirement.
RRSP	Registered Retirement Saving Plan is the name given to a private pension plan. It is a tax deferral plan which allows payments towards the plan to compound tax free until the funds are withdrawn. This plan ends at age 71.
RPP	This is an employer-sponsored pension plan and may be either a defined benefit or money purchase type.

Self-Directed RRSP	This is a registered retirement saving plan where you decide how you want your money invested. Your choice usually involves, Guaranteed Investment Certificates, Equity Funds, Mortgage Funds and Mutual Funds.
Short Term Objectives	These are tasks which aid one in achieving their goals and are usually accomplished in less than one year.
Short Term Goals	Usually referring to goals which will be accomplished in less than one year.
Tax Credit	The amount of money deducted directly from the amount of tax owing.
Tax Preparer	Someone or an organization who, for a fee, prepares your annual income tax return.
Tax Shelter	The creation of a tax loss to offset an individual's taxable income and in doing so reduce the amount of current tax payable.
Taxable Income	The amount of income after all deductions and credits have been applied. This is the amount on which tax owing is calculated.
Term Deposits	An amount of money held on deposit with a financial institution for a specific period of time at a fixed rate of return.
Term Insurance	Life insurance protection for a specific amount and has no savings built into the policy. It is straight protection.
Testamentary Trust	This is a trust which is included in a Will and becomes operational upon a person's death.
Tithe	A tithe is one-tenth. A biblical term used in the Bible to offer a guideline for giving.
Trust	This is an arrangement where you make provision for a trustee to oversee the management of assets for the benefit of someone else.
Trustee	A person appointed to carry out the responsibilities of a specific trust. An executor could be the trustee of your estate.
Variable Expenses	Expenses which are subject to change as a result of circumstances which are usually beyond our control.
Whole Life Insurance	Life insurance protection for a specific amount and contains a savings portion built into the policy. It may issue dividends to the policy holder.

Will   A legal document which provides for the settlement of
                            any liabilities and distribution of your assets after your
                            death. This is an important document and should be
                            prepared by a lawyer.

Year-End Tax Plan   The process of analyzing your tax situation for the
                            current year and determining action necessary to lower
                            your taxes.

Biblical References Pertaining To Finances

Business Virtues

Lev. 19:35,36; Dt.24:15, 25:15; Ps.1:1-3; 25:21; 37:37; 105:44,45; 112:6; 127:1,2; Pr.4:4, 5:21; 6:16-19; 10:4,5; 11:1,3,18,25-27; 12:7,22,23; 13:4; 14:23; 16:8,11; 18:9; 19:1; 21:3; 22:1,29; 28:6,13; Ecc.5:12; Jer.22:13; Mt.7:20; Ro.13:8; 1Co.4:2;

Budgeting

Pr.14:15; 22:3; 24:3,4; 27:12; Lk.12:16-21 14:28 30; 1Co.16:1,2;

Credit

Ex. 22:14; Dt. 15:8; 24:6; 2Ki.4:1; 24:3; Ps.37:21,26; 112:5; Pr.22:7; Mt.5:42; 18:24,25; Lk.6:35; Ro. 13:8;

Debt

Dt. 15:6,7; Dt. 28:11-14; Dt.24:6; 2Ki. 4:1,7; Job 24:9; Ps. 37:21; Ps. 112:5,9; Pr. 3:27,28; Pr. 6:1-3; Pr. 11:15; Pr. 17:18; Pr. 22:7, 26; Pr. 27:13; Ha.2:7; Lk. 7:42; Lk. 12: 58,59; Mt. 6:12; Mt.18:25, 27,30,32; Ro. 13:8;

Giving

Ru.2:15; Ps.112:9; Pr. 3:27; 11:10,15,24,25; 13:22; 14:21,31; 22:9; Isa.21:14; Mal. 3:7-10; Mt.5:42, 6:1,3,11,19,20,24; 10:8,42; 19:21; Lk.3:11; 6:38; 10:24,35; 11:41; 12:33; 18:22; 21:1 4; Ac.3:6; 4:34,35; 11:29; 20:35; Ro.12:8,13; 1Co.16:2; 2Co.8:3,12; 9:6,7; Gal.6:10; 1Ti6:18; Heb.13:16;

Planning

Ps. 37:23; Pr. 6:6-8; 13:11; 14:12; 15:22; 16:3,9; 19:21; 20:18,21; Mt.6:19; Lk.14:28-30; Jas.4:13-16;

Wealth

Dt.8; 28: 1-14; Ps.50:10-12; Pr. 3:9,10; 10:22; 11,4; 13:11,18,21; 18:11; 20:21; 21:21; 22:4; Ecc.5:12; Mt.6:19,24; Lk.12:16-21; 18:24; Php.3:8 1Ti.6:19;

Forms
For
Personal Use

SUMMARY ASSET EVALUATION FORM

ASSETS   LIABILITIES

ASSETS		LIABILITIES	
Chequing Accounts	$ _____	Bank Loans	$ _____
Savings Accounts	_____	Charge Accounts	_____
Life Ins. Cash Value	_____	Monthly Bills O/S	_____
Money Owed You	_____	Other	_____
Gold/Silver	_____		
Securities	_____	*Mortgages*	_____
Stocks	_____	Home	_____
Canada Savings Bonds	_____	Cottage	_____
Mutual Funds	_____	Other	_____
Term Deposits	_____		
Business	_____	Debts/Individuals	_____
Other	_____	Credit Unions	_____
		Personal Property Loans	_____
Automobiles	_____	Automobiles	_____
House Funishings	_____	Rec. Vehicles	_____
Antiques/Jewelry	_____	Other	_____
Real Estate	_____		
Home	_____	*TOTAL LIABILITIY*	$ _____
Cottage	_____		
Condo	_____		
Other	_____		
Pension	_____	*NET WORTH*	_____
Company	_____		
RRSP's	_____	Total Assets	$ _____
Annuities	_____	Less	_____
Insurance Face Value	_____	Total Liabilities	$ _____
Insurance FV Spouse	_____		
Other	_____	Net Estate	$ _____
TOTAL ASSETS	$ _____	Dated _____	

SOURCES OF ANNUAL INCOME

Annual Family Total

Present employment   _____

Spousal employment   _____

Part-time employment   _____

Investments   _____

Interest on money invested   _____

Money owed you   _____

Pension Company   _____

Pension Private   _____

Annuities   _____

RRIF   _____

Canada Pension   _____

Old Age Security   _____

Canada Pension Supplements   _____

Rental Income   _____

Other   _____

TOTAL INCOME $ _____

Anticipated Expenses

Fixed Expenses

Tithe	_____
Rent/Mortgage	_____
Insurance	_____
Bank Loans	_____
Health Insurance	_____
Saving Program	_____
Emergency Fund	_____
Other	_____
Total Fixed Expenses	$ _____

Variable Expenses

	_____
Food (At Home, Restaurants)	_____
Transportation (Ins., Gas, Fares)	_____
Clothing	_____
Recreation	_____
Vacations	_____
Utilities (Heat, Hydro, Water)	_____
Home Improvements	_____
Other	_____
Other	_____
Total Variable Expenses	$ _____
Total Expenditures	$ _____

THE FAMILY BUDGET

INCOME

Present Employment _____
Spousal Employment _____
Part-Time Employment _____
Investment Interest _____
Interest On Money Invested _____
Money Owed You _____
Pension Company _____
Private Pension _____
Annuities _____
RRIF _____
Canada Pension _____
Old Age Security _____
Canada Pension Supplements _____
Rental Income _____
Other _____
TOTAL INCOME $ _____

EXPENSES

Food $ _____
Shelter _____
Transportation _____
Emergency Fund _____
Entertainment _____
Recreation _____
Security _____
Charitable Donations _____
Utilities _____
Taxes _____
Debt Payment _____
Investments _____
Medical Expenses _____
Clothing _____
Personal _____
Other _____
TOTAL EXPENSES $ _____

Schedule 1

Purchase price of the home $ _____
Less
Available downpayment $ _____

Proposed mortgage amount $ _____

Schedule 2

Proposed monthly mortgage $ _____

Proposed monthly taxes $ _____

Total monthly payment $ _____

Schedule 3

New Home Operating Expenses

Monthly Mortgage	$ _____
Property Taxes	$ _____
Condominium Fees	$ _____
Utilities (Water, Hydro)	$ _____
Heating Costs	$ _____
Communications (Phone, Cable)	$ _____
Property Insurance	$ _____
Appliances	$ _____
Repairs/Renovations	$ _____
Tools (Lawn Mower, Shovels)	$ _____
Other	$ _____
Total Monthly Expenses	$ _____

Schedule 4

Available Cash

Money In Savings	$ _____
Canada Savings Bonds	$ _____
Canadian Securities	$ _____
Residue From Sale Of House	$ _____
Miscellaneous	$ _____
Other	$ _____
Total Cash Available	$ _____

Schedule 5

Moving Expenses

Moving Company	$ _____
Utility Deposits (Phone Hydro)	$ _____
Moving Equipment	$ _____
Packing Material	$ _____
Storage Costs	$ _____
Temporary Lodging	$ _____
Other	$ _____
Total Moving Expenses	$ _____

Closing Expenses

Lawyer's Fees	$ _____
Mortgage Fees	$ _____
Land Transfer Tax	$ _____
Adjustments (Fuel, Prepaid Taxes)	$ _____
Registration Fees	$ _____
Appraisal Fees	$ _____
Proposed GST	$ _____
Total Closing Costs	$

Notes

Notes

Speaking Engagements
And
Teaching Seminars

Monty McKinnon and/or the Master Financial Planning team is available for seminars or other speaking engagements throughout the year for Churches, para church organizations, special conferences and bible colleges.

Money Management For Busy People Newsletter

A newsletter is planned for release shortly. The purpose of this newsletter is to keep Christians informed about financial decisions affecting your life.

This is a financial newsletter, offered quarterly, which will present financial information from a biblical viewpoint. Designed to instruct and inform the reader of current tax planning strategies and a practical approach to handling money.

If you would like a sample of this letter, write to the address indicated below.

Please Write:

Master Financial Planning Services Inc.
P.O. Box 131
Newmarket, ON
L3Y 4W3

YES! I'm interested in a personal financial planning consultant coming to visit me at my convenience.

☐ In my home   ☐ In my office

Date Preferred _____   Time Preferred _____ AM
PM

Name: _____

Address: _____

City: _____ Prov: _____ Postal Code: _____

Phone: Home ( ) _____ Office ( ) _____

Birthdate: _____ Spouse's Birthdate _____

Areas of interest:

☐ Will Preparation/Review   ☐ Tax Planning
☐ Retirement Planning   ☐ Budgeting
☐ Seminar In My Area   ☐ Financial Planning
                              Newsletter

Att: Financial Planning Dept.

CROSSROADS CHRISTIAN COMMUNICATIONS INC.

100 Huntley Street
Toronto, Ontario
M4Y 9Z9